BRIDGING THE
CLASS DIVIDE

Bridging
THE
Class Divide

....

And Other Lessons for
Grassroots Organizing

....

LINDA STOUT

FOUNDER OF THE
PIEDMONT PEACE PROJECT

With a Foreword by Howard Zinn

BEACON PRESS · BOSTON

Beacon Press
25 Beacon Street
Boston, Massachusetts 02108-2892

Beacon Press books are published
under the auspices of the
Unitarian Universalist Association of Congregations.

Beacon Press gratefully acknowledges the support
of the Unitarian Universalist Veatch Program
at Shelter Rock.

01 00 99 98 97 96   8 7 6 5 4 3 2 1

Text design by Boskeydell Studio

Composition by Wilsted & Taylor

Library of Congress Cataloging-in Publication Data
can be found on page 194.

For my friend and sister in the struggle,
Cathy Hoffman

Contents

Foreword

LINDA STOUT'S STORY makes me think of other women in the history of this country—mostly unrecognized, their work unrecorded—whose roots are in the working class, and who have raised their voices above the clamor of academic conversation and boardroom conferences, speaking of equality and justice, demanding to be heard.

I think of the young women in the textile mills of Lowell, Massachusetts, in the 1830s, who formed a Female Labor Reform Association, put out "Factory Tracts," organized mass meetings, went out on strike, denouncing the "moneyed aristocracy" which controlled their lives.

I think also of Leona Barry, the Irish hosiery mill worker (Linda Stout also worked in a hosiery mill) who in the 1880s became an organizer for the Knights of Labor, appointed "to go forth and educate her sister working-women and the public generally as to their needs and necessities."

And there was Mary Ellen Lease, the fiery Populist orator, who spoke for farmers of North and South when she addressed the People's Party convention in Topeka in 1890: "Wall Street owns the country. It is no longer a government of the people, by the people and for the people...."

In this century, there arose working-class heroes like

Mother Mary Jones, who, in her eighties, went into the mining canyons of West Virginia and Colorado to support the struggle of mostly immigrant families against the feudal power of the robber barons. More recently, we have come to recognize the black women of the deep South, like Fannie Lou Hamer, who faced beatings and gunfire to work with the poor of the Mississippi Delta.

Linda Stout takes her own place in that long tradition of women leaders—in the antislavery movement, the Populist movement, the labor movement. Her work forms a link between that history and the struggles to come in the twenty-first century.

Her voice is not one we often hear, out of that mountain of books produced by educated men and women. She is a white (though with a Cherokee great-grandmother) working-class woman from North Carolina, whose parents were tenant farmers and mill workers with barely an elementary school education, yet attended Quaker meeting and raised their children to reject prejudice and violence.

It is a voice to listen to, because behind it is a unique experience from which we may learn what is absolutely essential for us to know at this moment in American history—how to begin to bring people together to create a decent society. Yes, that is what "organizers" do, and what all of us can do if we have the will. It is what Linda Stout set out to do in the Piedmont region against enormous odds, a story she recounts for us in this book.

Do we want to take down the walls that keep us apart—the differences of race, of sex, of class, of nation—to create conditions in which people can live in dignity, in peaceful neighborhoods, cities, countries, continents? That has been Linda Stout's dream—as it has been ours—but not just a dream, because she set out firmly, on the ground where she lived in the Piedmont region, to make a beginning.

She formed the Piedmont Peace Project, and after a while there were five hundred members, more blacks than whites, more women than men, almost all poor, and all determined to do something larger than to give social services to their community. Their aim was to bring about social change. In the course of that effort, they transformed themselves.

Linda Stout's book begins with her own story—poignant, troubling, fascinating—and continues with the story of the Piedmont Peace Project, how it began, how it came to be known far beyond the hill country of North Carolina. We learn from her own experience to think about something we tend to pass over quickly—how the language we use, as well as the barrage of "facts" we confidently present, can be either a stone barrier between working class and middle class, or a hedge over which we can leap if we try.

These pages contain precious wisdom on the most practical aspects of organizing, but also about holding to principles of fairness, and insisting that behind local problems are global ones (militarism, war)—an insistence some would call "impractical." We recall Martin Luther King's determination to speak out against the war in Vietnam, against all the "practical" advice of other leaders in the civil rights movement.

Linda Stout made a journey of self-education that took over a decade, and in passing on to us what she learned, she quickens our own learning. You read her book, you read her life, and you are encouraged to think about what people can do now to build the bridges we need to cross over together into the twenty-first century. You think about what you yourself can do, on whatever small spot of ground you occupy.

HOWARD ZINN

Preface

IT STILL SURPRISES ME that I have written a book. When I first began political organizing, I said I would do anything, except write! It wasn't that I hated writing; it was just that I "couldn't" write. Or at least, that was what I believed. Like many people in my situation, I believed the messages that society gave me: If I'm poor, it must be my fault. If I'm poor, I'm not important. I can't be as good as other people. I can't be smart or articulate. And, I certainly can't write a book!

At the same time that I began struggling to write a little (I had to learn to write foundation proposals and reports for my organization), I began to look at the ways growing up in poverty had affected my life. I began to understand differences between myself and people from other economic backgrounds. I started exploring issues of classism (a system of oppression that gives one group power and privilege over another group based on income and access to resources). I began to question my beliefs about myself and others like me, and through my questions I began to understand how the class system works and how pervasive it is in our society. As I came to understand that my "poverty" was not my fault or the fault of my parents,

I began to overcome the sense of inferiority I had been taught. I had to learn to be proud of who I was despite my poverty.

Through working to understand how poverty and classism oppress people, I found my own voice. Trusting my own voice meant overcoming both my fear of expressing my views and the feeling that I didn't deserve to be heard. The only people who have ever been able to understand these feelings have been those who have had to overcome the same barriers.

So, what does this have to do with writing? I began to understand that "our words" were important. That we, poor people, have things to say, and that we have knowledge that is crucial for the peaceful future of the world.

In my work, I speak two languages: one I use in my own community and family, and the other one I have had to learn in order to communicate with middle-class people. Unfortunately, my first language has not been seen as "equal." I have had to become "bi-lingual" in order to be accepted in a middle-class world. If I talk the way that comes most naturally to me, people judge me as being unintelligent or, at least, inarticulate. I no longer accept these judgments. In this book I speak in my own voice.

Acknowledgments

MANY PEOPLE have helped make this book a reality. I especially thank the Piedmont Peace Project staff, without whose contributions, ideas, and work there would have been no reason for a book: Delane Arnold, Tatia Ashe, Brenda Brown, Joan Bryant, George Friday, Maurice Jones, Connie Leeper, Susan Plyler, Laura Starkey, Estrella Soto, and Jesse Wimberley. I also want to thank the consultants and organizational mentors who worked with PPP: Dottye Burt-Markowitz, Pat Callair, Ron Charity, who died April 27, 1991, and Jane Wholey. In addition, I offer thanks to all the donors and volunteers of PPP who have made our dreams become a reality; and to Richard Brown, Corine Cannon, Marty Prince, Minnie Ray, to the memory of Kebie Hatcher and Jack McCorkle, I give thanks, as well as to all the rest of the members of PPP, whose names, if I gave them all, would fill a book.

I want to thank my friends Carol Dwyer and Robbie Kunreuther, whom I consider family and who supported me with their love and respect throughout the writing of this book. I also thank my friends Dottye Burt-Markowitz and Stan Markowitz for their help and advice with this book. I thank David

Foecke and Pat Close for their ongoing belief in me and support of my work over the past twelve years. And I give thanks to the friends who were the mainstay of my life during my year in Massachusetts: Chick Ackley, Sally Bubier, Loring and Louise Conant, Lynn Courtney, Carol Dwyer, Elly Bemis, Lynn Holbein, Pam Kelly, John and Susanne Potts, Laurie Schecter, and Roz and Tony Winsor. I also want to give special thanks to Cathy Hoffman, to whom this book is dedicated. She not only spent many hours reading, advising, and editing, but by encouraging, challenging, pushing, teasing, comforting, and most of all by believing in me, Cathy made sure this book was written.

I also thank Florence Ladd, director of the Bunting Institute, and the Radcliffe Public Policy Institute for their support during my year in Massachusetts.

I give thanks to the Carolina Community Project and its first director, Cathy Howell, with whom I spent hours talking, sharing our fears, hurts, and triumphs of finding our voices despite the classism we faced in our lives. I thank John Wancheck, as well, CCP's second director, who listened to me and offered advice with incredible patience and stamina.

I want to thank the assistants who helped me with transcription, research, and editing: Nancy Bates, Victoria Byerly, Joyce Mandel, Oclissha Miller, and Susan Plyler. And also to express my appreciation to Beacon Press and my editors who guided me through many rewrites and changes, Lauren Bryant, Marya Van't Hul, and copy editor Lydia Howarth.

I thank the staff of the Peace Development Fund, all of whom join me now in working to create a just and peaceful future: Juan Carlos Aguilar, Nancy Emond, Connie Fitzgerald, Lynne Gerber, Dana Gillette, Kenneth Jones, David Rogers, and Rose Sackey-Milligan.

I owe a great debt to my mentors and spiritual guides: Ron Charity, Septima Clark, my Cherokee great-grandmother, and my father, Herschal Stout.

And finally, I thank my mother, Kathleen Stout, whose unconditional love, support, and belief in me have never wavered.

Introduction

IN ORDER TO understand why I wrote this book you need to understand my vision for the future. It is this vision that has led me to work most of my life for social change and to begin to look at what I believe we, as a progressive movement, need to focus on.

I imagine getting up in the morning and breathing freely without the help of my daily medications for asthma. I walk out of my house into clean air that is pollution free. I greet people who are out walking that early in the morning with a sense of the real community we have built for each other. There are people of all ages and colors. On the way back to my house I visit the community garden and pick my share of organic food we have grown together.

In my vision, everyone has a job that they are able to do and enjoy. The jobs that no one wants are shared by everyone. There is time to spend together with family and community. We do not have to worry about the homeless and the hungry, because everyone who's able to work is provided with access to a good job and child care and those who aren't able are cared for. Everyone has health insurance and good medical care. We know that our children are getting a good multicultural education and everyone has access to the college or trade schools that they wish to attend. We do not worry that our world is going to blow up or that the ozone layer is becoming more depleted, and many of our group efforts are focused on cleaning up our world.

It's a world where different religions are honored, sexual orientation is respected, disabled people are allowed access to participate fully in society, as are the elderly and young. We have access to media that provide important information and present all different viewpoints. We live in a democracy where everyone's voice is heard and everyone has the opportunity to share in leadership.

This is my vision, and I think it's the vision of many others who work for a better world. Does it sound too idealistic or like science fiction? Maybe. But if so, I believe that is only because we have strayed too far from a country that is concerned with the needs of all its people and neared a country devoted to the profits of a few. Where we are currently headed is exactly the opposite of my vision. This present and future world is one where very few of us are strengthened by any healthy sense of community—even among our families. A world where we wake up every day knowing we have the capacity to destroy the world many times over with nuclear weapons and chemicals. Where every day our health is threatened by the air we breathe, the water we drink and bathe in, the foods we eat, and where our health risks increase at the same time that fewer and fewer people can afford adequate health care. This present and future world is one where violence continues to grow and we continue to build more jails in response, instead of putting our resources and energy into education and jobs for our youth. It's one where the dramatic increase in the disparity between rich and poor that we've experienced in the past few decades continues to drive us even farther apart, and current conflicts between races and classes escalate. Where we see even more homeless and hungry people, many of whom are children, sleeping on the streets and begging for help. And it is a world where almost no one believes that the political system works anymore.

If I believe this is the world we are heading for, why do I call myself an optimist? I do so because my vision of a different world persists and because I continue to work with others to turn us toward that vision. I believe we can make a difference. Yet, I believe that if we don't make radical changes in our society, we are truly on the verge of self-destruction. We are in serious crisis. We must work together to make real and lasting changes if we are to survive as families, as a community, and as a democracy ensuring equality and freedom for everyone. I also believe that we live in a time when we are on the verge of losing the opportunity to create a society that is based on democratic principles. *The time to make changes is now.*

How can we tell that past efforts to create real democracy in our nation have not succeeded? I think the evidence is all around us. Let's look at the fact that the civil rights and women's movements have successfully expanded the right to vote, yet millions of North Americans—from 50 to 75 percent, depending on the election—do not vote. While some people blame those who don't vote and those who don't even register to vote, a study of voting patterns strongly indicates that most nonvoters believe that they cannot influence those who govern them, whether at the local or national level.* If so many North Americans have so little faith in our political system or in our leaders, then we should examine the system. Before we explain away our citizens' failure to vote as apathy, we must explain why so many more people in other democracies do vote. People in the United States have limited faith that they can influence the government, and they believe that powerful interests—corporate and issue-oriented lobbies —influence government decisions and legislation. The evidence that North Americans are right in that judgment is overwhelming.

Not only have many poor, working-class, and increasingly middle-class North American voters lost faith in our political system, but our sources of information—so crucial to the health of a democracy—do not provide the information and insight necessary to help us understand what is going on and why so that we can vote intelligently. Increasingly, we find that television stations and newspapers are owned by corporations or powerful wealthy individuals. Do we seriously believe that a television station or newspaper owned by a corporation or someone interested primarily in profits, and having to compete in the economic marketplace, will do the job that it is required to do in a democratic society? The marketplace is not concerned with political democracies, it's concerned with profits.

---

* In the documentary film *The Rage for Democracy* (1991), Sidney Verba, professor of political science at Harvard University, notes that people from higher classes have a higher feeling of "voter efficacy"—they feel that their vote has an impact. The film, which reports findings of the Citizen Participation Project (a collaborative study and ambitious survey designed and executed by a number of political scientists) also indicates that poorer people with lower levels of education tend to feel that their vote does not make a difference, and that this feeling impacts voter turnout in those communities. See *The Rage for Democracy*, written, directed, and produced by Noel Buckner and Rob Whittlesey, © 1991 by William Benton Broadcast Project, University of Chicago.

Not only do the media reflect the pressures of the marketplace; they also reflect the interests of their owners and editors who are, most often, white and middle-class. We need only look at our own Constitution and Bill of Rights to get the point. These documents had some impressive features. For example, they spelled out many of the rules by which representatives of the people were to be elected, their terms of office, the limits of their power, and guaranteed freedom of religion, of speech, and of the press. But these documents were written by white, upper-class, Protestant men. Women, African Americans, poor and working-class Americans, and Native Americans had no role in creating the Constitution or Bill of Rights. These documents did not guarantee women the right to vote or to compete in the workplace with men, did not prohibit slavery, did not protect tribal territories, did not guarantee workers the right to organize and bargain for better wages, nor establish any programs to provide for the social security of workers or the poor. The men writing these important documents in the late eighteenth century did not speak for nor guard many of the basic interests of people then living in the United States. Nor do our media today speak for or effectively inform the majority of North Americans. Polls indicate that citizens don't trust the media to inform them accurately and adequately. And again they are right.

The 1980s witnessed the greatest transfer of wealth from the great majority of our citizens to the wealthiest 10 percent of North Americans. With that transfer of wealth went even greater influence over government decision making (through lobbyists, campaign funding, media control). The tax structure continues to dramatically favor wealthy Americans. CEOs in our companies make far more in relation to their employees than CEOs in any other industrialized country. The increased gap between the wealthiest 10 percent of North Americans and the rest of us is greater than the gap in all other industrialized countries. At the same time that wealthy Americans and North American corporations get more money and more power, most people are seeing the quality of their lives and their standard of living decrease. The great majority of our citizens are working substantially more hours for less pay. Higher paying jobs for most people are decreasing, and at the same time technology and the movement of companies to other countries are causing increased unemployment. For the first time in our history, polls show that a majority of U.S. citizens do not think that their children will be financially better off than they were. The American dream of owning a house, sending your children to college, having adequate and effective health care and retirement programs is being replaced by a nightmare of losing your home, not being able to afford higher education, facing catastrophic health costs, and having no money to set aside for the future.

Why do we assume we have a democracy when hard-working people cannot rely on the government and market-place to be concerned about fairness and the quality of their lives? The U.S. government and marketplace care little or nothing about leisure time for workers. To me it is incredible that every other European industrialized country and Japan offer workers from two to six weeks of vacation guaranteed by law—most often four to six weeks. We offer no guaranteed vacations. Thus, millions of Americans have no vacation, millions more have only one week and most have two or less. How does this fact reflect on our concern for the well-being of working people or for family values? Unlike other industrialized societies, our government and our corporations don't believe that working people deserve time for themselves and their families. What a commentary on the values of our society!

Census projections tell us that by the year 2056 over 50 percent of North Americans will trace their ancestry to a non-European country. Greater racial and ethnic diversity are here to stay. Yet racism seems to be getting stronger—just when we as a society need to figure out how to deal with differences. Increased economic problems will fall most heavily on people of color and women, and that will make the potential for racial and ethnic violence even greater.

We have many other serious problems in our society today but the lack of political power or trust, the lack of access to information, the degenerating economic condition of many North American families while a few increase their wealth and power, and the growing tensions around diversity in our society are, taken together, serious indications of a failure of democracy. Despite all our efforts, we aren't winning.

Many people have asked me what this means—"Who are 'we'?" The "we" is all of us in this country who want social justice and social change. We are women who face sexism in our daily lives and bear the economic burden of raising our children; we are poor people who want more jobs, fair wages, good working conditions, and access to the basic necessities of life, like housing, health care, and education; we are people of color who want to live in a society free of racism and with equal rights; we are gay men, lesbians, and bisexuals who want to live in a world that honors who we are and gives us equal rights; and we are all people who want to live in a safe world, free of nuclear weapons and war, and with a clean environment.

For years in the United States, tens of thousands of committed, caring people in the labor movement, the civil rights movement, the peace movement, and the women's movement, among others, have all struggled to create social change. And they have had many successes. *But throughout our history there has been no ongoing collective force that has been able to continually and successfully push for major societal change. As a result real change—political, economic, environmental, and social democracy—has not happened in our country and we are seeing the gains these movements have made being eroded daily.*

For instance, while the civil rights movement of the 1960s achieved many victories and changed many laws, institutionalized racism is still rampant. The right to vote was won but challenges to access to register and vote are still major issues in many parts of the country. We also see many gains made by the civil rights movement, such as affirmative action, now being challenged. The women's movement won the right to legal abortion but many poor women still lack access to abortion services, and legal abortion itself is being challenged in different states.

I believe that many of the groups struggling for social justice share similar goals, but these groups have not managed to work together effectively. Social justice begins with economic justice—but too often, social movements in this country are run by middle-class leaders (often white and male) who are not directly affected by the economic inequalities and other problems they are trying to solve. For most people of color, economic justice is critical, since racism in our society means a majority of people of color are low-income. Yet, too often, we see well-intentioned white folks make the mistake of analyzing problems that affect communities of color, making plans to address those problems, and then maybe (and only as an afterthought), bringing in people of color and asking for their support.

Economic justice is critical for all women too. While the women's movement has made lots of progress, women still lack equal pay and affordable child care, to name just two problems. These issues are especially critical for low-income women, many of them women of color, yet the women's movement is made up primarily of white, middle- and upper-class women.

The same is true for environmentalist and peace groups. While it is low-income people who are most directly affected by toxic waste dumping and by unsafe environmental conditions in the workplace, the environmental movement is mostly middle-class and white. Similarly, in the peace movement, even though the military budget's drain on resources for human needs most directly affects poor communities, the recognized leaders tend to be middle-class white men and women.

A further problem hampering social reform is that most reformers are issue oriented—they want to deal with a particular problem in society. They may want to reform prisons or guarantee reproductive choice or increase gun control. These are all important objectives but they are founded on single issues, which makes it more difficult to build a broad base of support, especially in low-income communities.

Of course, there have been many really progressive organizations in this country that recognize that only when we have major social, political, and economic change will North Americans gain the political power and the economic and social justice that is necessary in a truly democratic society. But these organizations have always had to face hostility from powerful institutions, the government, law enforcement, the business community, and the media—hostility that has hindered their efforts. They have always had to struggle for financial resources. Their staffs have been subject to constant stress due to these obstacles, threats of violence, constant lack of money, and strain on relationships and family.

All of these obstacles have prevented progressive organizations from making successful social change. Yet other obstacles have hindered them as well. Too often, they have failed to organize across class, race, and gender lines (which means not only bringing in diverse members but also constantly working to enable a diverse group to work together); to find alternative sources of funding; to learn to use the media to their advantage; to help people in communities understand the connections between local and national issues; to recognize that staff members need a decent income, vacation, health care—just like people in the marketplace; and to adopt useful practices from other institutions.

Piedmont Peace Project, based in North Carolina, is a grassroots organization that has developed a different kind of model for organizing work, one that has enabled PPP to overcome many of the obstacles that have hindered other progressive groups. PPP is primarily made up of poor people—the members, the board of directors, and the staff. They work in a large central rural region of North Carolina, a twelve-county area that's about the size of the state of Massachusetts. Most members work in the textile mills, farm, or do domestic work. The organization is approximately 70 percent people of color, and a majority are women. Young people are also a big part of the organization since you can't organize low-income folks without including their children. The average reading level in the district for adults is third grade, and over half of the constituency has no high school education. Several of the leaders in the organization can't read.

While PPP organizes by going door-to-door on the issues that affect people in the communities—housing, water and sewer, economic development, health care—PPP also educates and organizes to connect the local concerns to broader national public policy issues. PPP builds power through its voter registration and "Get-Out-the-Vote" program, as well as by teaching the membership how to hold elected officials accountable.

At the Piedmont Peace Project we have learned a lot from the efforts of activists who have worked in the past and still work for change. We value and have tried to pattern ourselves after some of their successes. We have also tried to learn from their failures and we have tried to understand why this nation has never created the democratic society that we have said we want. The organizing model we have developed at PPP reflects what we believe social activists need to do to bring about a democratic revolution—real social change at last.

1

Growing Up Poor

IN THIS BOOK, I tell some of my own personal history in order to help you understand how poverty and North America's attitudes toward poor people disempower and oppress them. I tell my story in order to give you an understanding of how powerful and destructive oppression is in this country. If we are going to build a peaceful world, we must understand and address oppression as part of any work we do.

When my mother, Kathleen Arsula Hooper, was young, she was tall, with thick black hair and high cheekbones, characteristic of her Native American grandmother who was a Cherokee. Mama liked to read, and she was a feminist for her time— fiercely independent, even after she was married. My daddy came home once and noticed that Mama had painted her fingernails red. He did not like the red polish and told her to take it off. So the next day when he came home, she had painted not only her fingernails but her toenails and the rims of her eyeglasses. My father never said another word about it—and he was a wise man for it.

Mama's family was from the mountains, from Silva, North Carolina—Appalachia—where she grew up as one of nine children. They were poor. She has told me stories about having to go barefoot to school. Her father worked in a furniture factory in the mountains and her mother stayed at home with all the children. My mother only went through the seventh grade, but she loved to read. After she was married and we came along, she educated herself by reading all our books until we got to high school math—she skipped that—but she read everything else all the way through our schooling and educated herself that way.

My father's name was Herschal Joseph Stout, and he was from Asheboro, which is in the center of the state of North Carolina. He came from a family of subsistence farmers and from a long, long line of Quakers—the common name for people who are part of the religion of the Society of Friends. My father went through the sixth grade and worked as a tenant farmer. Quakers have traditionally been in the forefront of working for human and civil rights and against war and violence. My father was a pacifist—although he used guns for hunting food as most rural people did—and he taught us nonviolence. One time, I remember him being really angry with me—the angriest I ever remember him—because I was pretending to shoot someone with my finger.

I was sent to Friends Meeting in my community every Sunday. My father went once in a while but most of the time stayed home to take care of my mother. I usually went by myself and later with my younger sisters. As a child, Quaker Meeting meant *everything* to me. I learned so much there. We had a small children's group and a wonderful teacher. We loved her so much because she let us decide what we wanted to learn about and helped us do it. It was very empowering for us. Once a month we would present a program to the entire

Meeting. These were usually plays about historical figures in Quaker history, like William Penn and how he made peace with Native Americans, or someone who organized for women's rights in the 1800s or was part of the Underground Railroad helping slaves escape to freedom. Every year, when our class moved up to another level in First-Day school (what most churches call Sunday School), our teacher would move with us. At one point, the elders of the Meeting decided that we had developed too strong an attachment to this one teacher. They decided it was in our best interest to move on to another teacher. We children organized a protest during the Quaker Meeting: we stood up in the back of the Meeting and wouldn't sit down. When the adults realized what it was all about, they gave in to us on the issue of keeping our teacher. It was my first experience of using collective power to make change.

Ours was a very old and socially conservative, silent Meeting. Once it had been politically active, during the antislavery movement, as many of the Quaker meetings in the South had been. During the Civil War many southern Quaker men refused to fight, both because they were pacifists and because they opposed slavery. Many men in our community, including two of my great-grandfathers, hid from the Confederate military officers who went from house to house to draft men into the army. My great-aunt wrote in a letter that the Confederate soldiers had taken her and other women in our community out of their homes and smashed their fingers on the split rail fences in an attempt to make them tell where the men were hiding. To escape this and other forms of brutality, many southern Quakers and a lot of our family fled the area. The Quakers who remained became less politically active and focused more on their own community.

Even though I did not really learn political action from the Quaker Meeting, I did learn the rich history of Quakers who had worked for and even risked their lives for their beliefs. I also was taught the moral values of equality and justice that are now the basis for my political action. It was this background that influenced how I later dealt with my anger at the injustices that resulted from growing up poor.

My mother and her family were Southern Baptist. Even though we were Quakers, I was closer to my mother's family than to my father's. They were a spirited group always singing and having a good time. Mama's family accepted my father immediately. Everyone really loved him. My father's family had a hard time with the fact that he married a "mill-town girl" who was not a Quaker.

The first place I remember living was in my grandmother's attic—a place where Quaker men had hidden to avoid the draft during World War I. We lived with my father's mother because my parents could not afford a place of their own, and my father's two sisters and their families lived there as well. The house had no water or bathroom, was heated by a wood fire, and had limited electricity for lights. This was a difficult time for my mother because she was not accepted by my father's family and yet we were dependent on them for a place to live. By then, my sister Renae had been born, and I was five years old.

One night, in 1959, we had gone to visit friends of my parents. On the way home, a drunk driver going about a hundred miles an hour hit our car head on. My mother's leg was nearly severed. My father was thrown out of the car. The car was on fire. My little sister was cut badly on her face and temple and was screaming her head off, and I had a concussion.

Finally, an ambulance driver came and put me in the front

seat of the ambulance. We drove into Asheboro and I got to push the button that made the siren go. At the hospital, the doctor just looked at me and said I was fine. They didn't do any kind of checkup. I remember asking for chewing gum because my throat hurt (it was scorched from the fire), and everybody just laughed at me for asking for gum at such a serious time.

Instead of being admitted to the hospital, I was sent home with my uncle, a man I was afraid of because I knew he beat his kids, my cousins. I remember that there was nobody but me and this uncle in the house. I was very scared and very thirsty. I was begging for water but my uncle wouldn't give me any. And I kept telling him I was going to die. This uncle had a living room with a closet that had stairs up to the attic, and when I'd play there with my cousins, they used to scare me by telling me that monsters lived at the top of the stairs. Now he locked me in that room, and he threatened to beat me with a belt if I didn't shut up. I remember lying down and crying and thinking that I was going to die. That's the last thing I remember until I woke up in the hospital. During the night I had hemorrhaged from a fractured skull and had almost died.

My sister, Renae, remained in the hospital for over a month and then went to live with relatives for most of the next two years. When I finally saw my parents, they were both in casts. My mother was two weeks pregnant at the time of the accident, and there was a big discussion about whether to abort or not. The doctor told my father that either way, they didn't expect my mother to live. She had six or seven operations during the period while she was pregnant, and when she came out of the hospital she had only one leg, her thick black beautiful hair had turned white, and she had a baby, my sister Jane, whom she would never be able to carry. This was 1960, and she was thirty years old.

The people whose car had hit us got a lawyer, and before my parents were even out of the hospital, the other driver's wife had sued her husband in order to transfer everything into her name. My parents were told that there was nothing they could do to win damages from the man who hit us, and they didn't have the resources to get an attorney to advise them otherwise. Their lack of money for legal advice not only kept my parents from knowing what their options were; it also effectively deprived them of services they were entitled to.

Right after my father got out of the hospital, he bought a little trailer for us to live in. It was only ten feet by forty feet, baby blue with a streak of silver, but I thought it was the greatest thing on earth. Daddy was working then on farms as a hired laborer and at a place that put in furnaces. He had to borrow the money, since we got nothing from the accident. I was so excited because it was a brand-new trailer and it had a bathroom. We didn't have running water, so we couldn't use the bathroom, but, still, I was very proud of having it. The trailer also had two bedrooms, so there was one full bed for me, Renae, and later my sister Jane. And there was a tiny bedroom for my parents.

My mother's hospital bed was set up in the middle of the living space of our tiny trailer. Her leg was cut off two weeks after my sister Jane was born. The doctors apparently just whacked it off—what they called guillotine surgery. They didn't even cap any of the nerves. She eventually got a prosthesis, but it was incredibly painful and very difficult to use. She never had the freedom to walk like most people who have a prosthesis. The doctors said the amputation had been done in this way because they didn't think she would ever walk again, but I believe that if my parents had not been poor, my mother would have gotten much better medical care. Because my parents were never able to buy a wheelchair (she got one only later, when we girls were grown up and worked to buy her one), my mother never was able to go anywhere. For me it meant she didn't go to important events in my life—like my first day of school or to my graduation from high school. I know that my father was still paying hospital debts from the wreck when I was in high school, and for several years after that. My parents paid all those debts, but it took the rest of my father's life to do it.

After we were all back together again as a family in the trailer, my father would get up early and leave a sandwich and bottles for my baby sister Jane beside the hospital bed for my mother and then leave for work. She couldn't get up so she took care of Jane all day long in the bed with her. I very quickly became a major caretaker for Jane because Mama couldn't even carry her. I started cooking and washing dishes when I was so little that I had to stand on a stool to reach the sink. My mother would tell me word for word what to do from her hospital bed. I became her legs, a parent for my sisters, and my father's helper, and then I would go to school.

I was very excited about school. What I remember about that period was that I didn't have much contact with my parents because my father was working so much, and my mother was sick. It was a lonely time. I know my mother got angry often, and she cried a lot. To avoid thinking about the tension and problems at home, I focused more on Quaker Meeting and school.

I excelled in school in the first, second, and third grades

with straight A's, even though my teachers always said I talked too much. I had announced in the first grade, and reaffirmed every year after, that I was going to go to college and become a teacher when I grew up. I was used to being top in my class, always making the best grades and being considered one of the "smartest." But over and over, I came face to face with people's prejudice against me because my family was poor. My best friend all through school told me in the third grade that she couldn't come home and spend the night with me because her daddy said I was "white trash." I was incredibly hurt and confused by this, though I didn't know what it was about. That's when I first started feeling bad about myself, feeling I had done something wrong. I now realize this is an experience shared by countless low-income children.

The year I was in fourth grade, everything changed. One day my teacher called me to the board to do a division problem which she had not yet explained to us. I didn't know how to do it. When I told her I couldn't do it because she hadn't explained it yet, she told me in front of the whole class that I was stupid, that I would never make anything of myself, and that I might as well quit thinking of ever going to college. At that point, she moved me from the advanced group to the "lower less-achieving" group. From that day on, I never made good grades again at that school. I went from an A+ student to a C and D student from then until the eighth grade. And I never spoke in class. My teachers never again had to say I talked too much because I never said another word. Because of my own experience and seeing the same kinds of things happening now, I believe that telling children they can't do things becomes a self-fulfilling prophecy. I began to feel really bad about myself and to believe I couldn't succeed.

Before I entered eighth grade in 1968, we moved to Wood-leaf, North Carolina, so my father could get a job working in a textile plant, and I began the year in a new school. I still held onto the dream of going to college and being a teacher even though I was making average grades. I'm not sure why I held onto this dream in spite of all the discouragement I got along the way, but I did, and even before I got to high school, I knew I was going to have to make better grades if I wanted to go to college. I would have to get high enough grades to win schol-arships because my parents would not be able to afford college tuition. I had never felt good about being an average student. I knew I had the ability to do better. But I had to overcome my fear of failing, overcome the message I had been given that I couldn't succeed. I also had to overcome my fear of speaking in class since we were graded on class participation. I knew I had to start asking questions about things I didn't know in order to understand the information. I would stay awake at night worrying about how I was going to have to start talking in class.

Finally, I decided that I would watch how this one guy in class did it. His name was Stan. He was very popular and was considered very smart. He always talked in class and the teacher always listened to him. So I learned how to do what he did. One thing I realized right off was that he would speak out whether he knew an answer or not. That was a whole new concept for me; that someone would actually speak out not knowing something, that it could be wrong and still be okay. Stan did it, and he did not get called stupid in front of the whole class. I decided I was going to have to start speaking out, but unlike Stan, I felt that I had to know the right answer, so I studied hard. I would study lessons ahead of time—ahead of the class so that when we had class discussions, I would know what was coming up. I was afraid, but also very determined. I started speaking a little bit at a time, but the main thing was that I just started paying attention to building up my confidence. It really paid off! In one six-week period, I went from being an average C student to being an A+ student again.

After I started making good grades, I began thinking more and more about college. When it came time to sign up for high school, I went to see the school counselor and told her I wanted to sign up for college preparatory classes. In our discussion about what courses I should take, she gave me the choice of taking either American history or Bible. Now I had been taking Bible in elementary school because the Bible teacher came and taught us in class twice a week. It was unofficially required by the school, although students could get out of taking Bible class if their parents wrote them a note. So I decided to take Bible instead of American history, since all my friends were. I had no idea that Bible was not a college entrance requirement and that American history was, and the counselor made no attempt to explain it to me.

On my first day in high school, I realized that the counselor had signed me up for a home economics class. Since I had done housework all my life, I felt that I didn't come to school to learn home economics. I refused to take the class, and it was a scandal. Finally, I was assigned to a study class where we were expected to sit silently and do nothing for a whole hour. So, in my freshman year, at the age of fifteen, I had lost two classes toward college, history and the college-preparatory class that I could have taken in place of home economics. And I soon realized that the school counselor had assigned me to all basic courses instead of pre-college requirements. I was horrified. I started causing a scene about it. It required a major fight for me to take algebra and geometry the next year. Finally, I convinced the school to let me double up on all my classes to make up for the first year of high school, which could have been a setup for failure. But I didn't fail. I was in the National Honor Society and on the honor roll the entire time.

Even though I always talked about going to college, I had to fight for every piece of information on how to do it. Now, when I try to explain how difficult it was for me to get information about college, people often say, "Well, didn't they have a 'college day'?" "College day" in my school meant that the counselor selected certain students to be excused from class to talk to college recruiters. I never spoke to a college recruiter or even knew that they came to our school. I remember finding out about taking the Standard Achievements Test (SAT) barely in time to be considered for college. And that hasn't changed much in North Carolina. Working-class students are still often kept in the dark about how to get into college. My high school counselor knew that I wanted to go to college, and she never helped me. Finally, though, I graduated and won a scholarship to Lenoir Rhyne College in Hickory, North Carolina. In 1972, when I was eighteen, I left for college with the idea of majoring in mathematics.

Being a math major was an intensive course in sexism even though I didn't realize it at the time. I was in classes with almost all men, since few women were encouraged to major in math. I was often ignored in class and my questions were treated with disdain, even though I was often the one that other students turned to for help and tutoring with their assignments. I even got called to task and reprimanded for designing (and sharing!) a computer program to work our homework problems for us.

I liked math, and I did okay in it, but after taking a course in "communications," I realized that what I really enjoyed was presenting information that I had an interest in through writing and other methods. I had taken English in high school, but I never wrote in the so-called "correct" way, or in the language of a white middle-class person. What I now know is that I was writing in my own language. I was never able to adapt to standard English. It never felt right. I spoke my own working-class English then as I do now, although now, having worked with middle-class people, I have learned to use middle-class English, but it is not natural to me. I know a few low-income people who are able to easily move back and forth; they go into the middle-class community and are able to speak like middle-class people, but in their own communities they often continue to use working-class English. College often helps low-income people be able to do that.

In college, my working-class English was not acceptable. I remember in a communications course we were assigned a multimedia project, and my two projects—one on the environment and the other on women's voices—were rated the best by students in the class. However, I did not make a good grade because I didn't conform to standard English. It was a shock to me that I didn't get better grades because I knew I was doing good work and deserved high marks. But, at the same time, I also believed the teachers who claimed my way of speaking was inferior. Through experiences like this one in college, I lost much of my confidence in being able to speak publicly or write.

I did make good enough grades to keep my scholarship. Then, during my second year of college, another blow fell. My boarding cost was increased by five hundred dollars. My scholarship did not cover the extra cost and I didn't have the money. Another catch was that students were not allowed to have jobs that were not part of their awards package. If a student got a job, the amount of money earned was deducted from his or her scholarship. Since students had to get approved to make extra money, I tried to do that. But, according to them, my father made enough money to give me the extra five hundred dollars. Now, my father wasn't making a whole lot of money at the mill, and he was still paying off all the medical expenses from the car accident. He did try to go get a loan of $500 so he could give me the money, but he was turned down because he had no collateral. The trailer my family lived in was considered of no value. I will never forget the pain in his face when he was turned down and I kept asking him why and what was I going to do. I remember going back into the college financial aid office begging and crying for them to give me this money but they just wouldn't do it.

Finally, I decided to leave school. I sold my books, packed up, and got a job in the hosiery mill there in Hickory. Later that fall someone from Lenoir Rhyne College called to ask me why I hadn't come back. I couldn't believe it. I said, "What do you mean why am I not coming back? We had this discussion already and you said no to helping me come up with the money." They said, "We didn't know you were going to drop out." To which I said, "Well, I didn't drop out, I got forced out. You said you wouldn't give me the money, and I assumed that was what you meant." "Come in and talk to us, and we'll see what we can work out," they said. But, at that point, I had already moved off campus, got a job, and sold everything I owned. It was too late to talk about school. I didn't have the resources to change my life back to being a student at that point.

I was so angry at them, and I still am. For years, I thought it was somehow my fault that I didn't stay in school. When I tell this story to middle-class folks, they ask, "Well, why didn't you do this?" or "Why didn't you do that?" "Why didn't you try to get this kind of loan?" or "Why didn't you go to another college?" But at that time I did not know what other options were. I believed I had no other options available to me.

I have a card on my desk, and there's a picture of a basket with one egg in it. Under the picture it reads, "Sometimes you have to put all your eggs in one basket." With all the knowledge I have now, I could have figured out how to transfer to a cheaper school or found some other solution. But back then I did not know the first thing about options. I often define poverty as a lack of options. What I became aware of early on was that for me and other low-income people, many doors are closed. I didn't start out thinking that was true. But it is. Middle-class people have often challenged me about why I didn't try to go to another school or get other kinds of help. They believe that if I had really wanted to continue, I would have found a way. They don't understand that it is a privilege to have options, and that a lot of people don't have that privilege. They also cannot understand the intense pain and shame of not having those options available to you, and as a result, the sense of being a failure that it instills in you.

After I left college, at first I lived in a trailer with several other women while I worked in the Hickory hosiery mill. Later I got a job in the office at a manufacturing company in

Hickory and started looking for my own apartment. All the ads in the newspaper for apartments that I could afford read "Married couple or men only." I couldn't believe it! I will never forget one woman who told me when I called, "Well, honey, I would really like to rent to you but it's just not a good thing for a woman to live by herself." One person actually told me that they did not rent to women because they might commit immoral acts in their apartments. It was unbelievable to me that people could feel this way.

Before this time, even though I'd been aware of sexism, I'd never felt directly affected by it. I was somewhat aware of the feminist movement and its fight for equal pay, and while I agreed with that, I had never gotten involved. I also knew that some of my father's family did not like the fact that my mother was such a powerful voice in the family. But I didn't think that was the way the real world thought. So I was not prepared when I went apartment hunting and ended up having to get my boss to call someone he knew to help me get an apartment.

During the next few years I became for the first time acutely aware of sexism, racism, and homophobia at the places I worked and among my friends and extended family. My parents had taught me that prejudice was wrong, and I grew up without realizing how serious these problems were in our society. My biggest interest was in not being poor. I wanted to have a house and nice things. I wanted to be middle-class. But gradually that ambition clashed with the values I had learned growing up. I was torn between getting ahead and doing what I felt was right, for the price of getting ahead often meant having to go along with my employers' values by not questioning racist and sexist policies. But eventually my need to stand up against what I felt was wrong and to fight for justice became a much stronger force. Because of my personal experiences, I became more aware of the lesson that I had been taught as a Quaker, that not one of us could be free until all people could be free. This lesson moved me to begin to take very unpopular stands on the job and among some of my friends and family. I was working as an office manager in Hickory at the time, and I decided to hire African Americans and gay men. This decision made a lot of people unhappy, including my employer and some of my fellow workers, but I refused to go back on the principles of equality and justice I'd learned as a child. I was harassed and threatened, and finally I decided I had to move away. So, at the age of twenty-three, without the college education I'd dreamed of and very little money in my pocket, I went looking for what I hoped would be a better job and a place where I would begin to feel at home.

2

Becoming an Activist

IN THE FALL OF 1977, I moved to Charleston, South Carolina, with my sister Jane. My first job in Charleston was in a large family business—an insurance and rental company that owned a lot of property in Charleston—and it plunged me immediately back into the struggle of confronting prejudice and discrimination. My supervisor there told me that, if a black person called about renting an apartment, I was to tell them that we didn't have any openings. I was afraid to protest openly, but I figured out a way to resist those instructions. I just pretended that I could not tell if the person on the phone was black or white, although African Americans in Charleston tend to have a strong, recognizable accent. Because I claimed that I couldn't tell if callers were white or black, they took me off the phones.

One of the owners came in one day and was talking to one of the managers. They were laughing about the fact that a black family had moved onto the island where they lived and had been harassed by their white neighbors. Racist epithets had been painted on the black family's garage door. My bosses were laughing about running these black folks off the island.

After listening to them, I quit even before I had found another job.

I had learned bookkeeping and office management skills, so I decided to apply for a job I heard about in a law office. When I got to the law office, they gave me a test for secretarial skills. The first typing test I took, I typed only thirty-five words a minute with three mistakes. The lawyers interviewed me anyway, and I could tell that they liked me. They liked the fact that I was Quaker. One of them was Quaker, and they had both been conscientious objectors during the Vietnam War. So during the interview we talked politics. It was exciting to talk to them and realize that I could work for people who cared about the same kinds of things I did: equal rights for everyone and justice for those who were underprivileged. I had never had a job that was in line with my own beliefs as a Quaker. In fact, I had never even heard of civil rights attorneys. At first, the attorney told me he couldn't give me the job because I lacked the skills they needed. I left feeling devastated. But an hour later, he called me and offered me the job. He said he was interested in having someone who cared about the politics of the job and would give me a "test" period to learn the skills. I learned a lot in that job about injustice and the failure of our justice system in addressing the many wrongs I witnessed. I also worked for a wonderful man who always believed in me and, as a result, my self-confidence and the belief that I could do something began to grow.

The Charleston neighborhood I lived in then was right outside a military base and was not a safe place for two young women. My sister and I were so poor that first year that we both had to sell our cars and take public transportation. A lot of folks tried to warn us that riding the buses was "dangerous." Friends and the folks I worked with in the insurance and rental company were horrified at the idea of us riding the buses because white folks "just did not ride the buses" in that area. But we built strong friendships with people on the bus, including the bus drivers. I remember one time, a driver who had become a friend picked us up after we had been at the beach all day and had got sunburned. He drove off of his route to a drugstore and waited while we went in and bought Solarcaine. There were only two or three times when we had problems on the bus. Because the regulars on the bus knew us, they always took care of us. One day a man came on the bus and started hassling me. I was petrified. I didn't know what to do, and he was right in my face screaming and threatening me. Suddenly, the bus stopped and this man was literally thrown off. Before I knew what had happened, I was looking out the rear bus window seeing this man sitting in the middle of the road. While it was true in some ways that we lived in a dangerous neighborhood, riding the buses was for us a very positive and safe experience. White peoples' notion that riding the buses was unsafe because of black folks was simply prejudice, and in fact was totally untrue.

The Charleston buses I rode went through the low-income communities. Unlike other cities I've used public transportation in, the buses in Charleston were used mainly by low-income people, most of them black. One day because the bus was ahead of schedule, we were sitting awhile outside the projects. I saw a black man running down a hill toward the projects with two white policemen chasing him. He ran about halfway down the hill, and then, he stopped, turned around, and held up his hands. The policemen kept running toward him, knocked him down, and kicked him in the head. One stepped onto the man's back. They just kept beating him, even when he was on the ground. I started to jump off the bus to go to his defense, when people on the bus grabbed me. I was fighting them to get off the bus to help this man get away from these policemen who were beating him mercilessly. I had to stand there with the bus driver holding me and watch them brutally beat this man who had turned around and held his hands up.

I don't know what the man had done, if he had done anything. I looked in all the local papers for something about what happened to him, but nothing was ever reported about it. I never knew what happened to him, and I began to believe that the justice system was not to be trusted.

At work, I saw people come into the law office who had been beaten by the police. We would take pictures of their injuries. These cases would go to court, and even though they were substantiated with evidence, we would often lose a case because a judge wouldn't allow the jury to hear certain information or facts that would have supported the case. I remember a particular case where an innocent man was held by police and beaten. Their defense was that it was a "high drug area" and therefore they had the right to stop our client. Our law office had researched the area for all drug arrests in the past few years and had discovered that in fact it was not a drug or high crime area. But we were not allowed to present our research in court. Witnessing again and again that kind of failure of justice in the courts made it clear to me that something was badly wrong with our justice system.

During these early years in Charleston, I was continuing to struggle with sexual discrimination in every aspect of my life—from trying to get credit and access to housing to attitudes among friends, acquaintances, sales people, doctors. I became interested in the Equal Rights Amendment (ERA) and the women's movement. I believed the ERA was a way to work for equality for everyone and that it linked many of the problems that troubled me—sexism, racism, poverty. I discovered a group of women in Charleston who were organizing to pass the ERA and working for abortion rights. I began to go to their meetings and volunteer to help, but I always felt like an outsider. In fact, I felt stupid the entire time I was a part of that group.

Looking back I realize I could have done good work as part of this group, but they didn't value what I had to offer. I was interested in communicating to women like me, low-income women, in ways that they could understand. I knew that helping low-income women see the connections between poverty and discrimination that I had seen would be critical in building enough support to pass the ERA amendment. But when I volunteered to, for example, speak to women in the low-income community where I lived, I was ignored. Or when I volunteered to staff a table at an event or in a mall, I was told the organization would call me but I would never hear from them. Then, at the next meeting, someone else—invariably middle-class—would report having done what I'd volunteered to do.

No one in the women's group actually ever said that they didn't want me to do the things I offered to do, but that was the message I got. What became clear was that the group had already formed opinions about what low-income women wanted and did not believe low-income women would support a feminist agenda. I disagreed and believed we should be doing outreach to low-income women. I felt that I especially could reach them because I came from the same background. Probably because I was low-income, didn't speak "right," and wasn't college-educated, I couldn't persuade the women's group to my point of view. They couldn't hear what I said as valuable, and I wasn't yet able to see myself as capable of doing this work on my own. I began to feel discouraged and soon dropped out of the women's group, even though in many ways the group represented my own goals and beliefs.

After my brief encounter with the women's movement, I kept looking around for organizations and activities that were connected to my growing political beliefs. Eventually I got interested in the peace movement. By 1980 I had helped to start a Friends Meeting in Charleston, which had not had a Meeting for more than a hundred years, probably since the Civil War. As the Charleston Meeting became stronger, I grew more interested in the peace movement and wanted to become more active. The national peace movement had become more visible and a lot of information was coming to the Friends Meeting. As I learned more about nuclear weapons and military spending, I became more convinced that I needed to work on these issues also.

Our Friends Meeting had received requests from young men for a military draft counseling service. As I talked to people, I began to realize that a lot of young people joined the military because it was their only way to get an education and jobs. Many saw the military as their only way out of poverty, even though they did not believe in war or killing. I decided to get training through a national program on how to start a military draft counseling service and how to counsel. I asked the Meeting to sponsor it.

My effort to begin this counseling service taught me an important lesson about how to respond to disagreement by using patience, respect, and education. A couple of men who had joined our Meeting were not pacifists. One had retired from the military. He was an African American man who had joined the Friends Meeting because of its history of opposing slavery in Charleston. His military experience went against the idea of Quaker pacifism, though, and he would not support my efforts to begin draft counseling. In Quaker Meeting we use consensus to make decisions—which meant, in this case, that so long as this man objected, I could not start a military counseling service. I was horrified that someone could come in and stop the work that Quakers had always stood for, but that is the process in Quaker Meeting. I brought it up constantly at every business meeting and would argue about it. In anger, I finally decided to give up and not raise the subject again.

Soon after I had decided to back down, at our annual retreat, this man brought up the military counseling issue. He said, "You know, I understand when it is someone's conviction not to serve in the military and I support that, but what I can't support is that we would be encouraging people to break the law by giving them information on how to be a conscientious objector."

There was another person at the Meeting retreat who had studied the history of the Quakers. He pointed out that the question of whether to break the law to maintain traditional values had long been debated among Quakers. Historically, Quakers had decided that one must follow the "Inner Light," and that could mean having to break the law because the "Inner Light" is a higher law. He said Quakers had struggled with this issue of breaking the law when they decided to teach

Charleston slaves to read and write. He pointed out that Quakers had taught Nat Turner how to read and write when it was illegal to help any slave become literate. Afterwards, this African American man decided he would no longer block my efforts to organize a military draft counseling service. I never said a word. But that retreat taught me an important lesson in patience and about people's processes of change. I learned how important it was to hear people's concerns and fears, instead of challenging them with my beliefs. I also discovered the importance of education—especially a knowledge of history—in helping people gain a context for their beliefs and learn to make connections. Most of all, I saw the need for us to really listen and share our personal feelings with each other.

My experiences in the Friends Meeting taught me a lot about working in a group and about the kinds of injustice I wanted to fight against. But it was only when I began to think about how poor people are affected by national military spending that I found the route I wanted to take to make social change happen. I had heard about the peace movement's position on nuclear weapons, but I was mostly concerned about the rising cost of the military budget and the effect it was having on the economy. I kept reading and hearing in different publications that were sent to the Quaker Meeting about how much money was going into the military budget and how much waste there was in the government. Charleston has a naval base, a missile base, and an air force base. Sometimes I would visit friends who lived on the bases and would go to the elaborate open house events where the military showed off its equipment and resources. The local news carried lots of stories about government contracts and how much money was being spent for the military. I began to notice how all these piles of money went to the bases, while the people who lived next door to me in a run-down housing project were struggling to survive.

At first I just observed. I did not have all the facts in the form of statistics or figures. I just knew it the way a lot of low-income folks know it. When you see and hear about billion-dollar contracts while you're living in poverty, you know that something isn't right. If you go into the low-income community and talk to people, most will already be aware of excessive military spending without knowing any specific numbers. For one thing, low-income people have family members and friends in the military, and they know about all this waste. Almost any family who has a member in the military stationed at Fort Bragg in North Carolina will tell you many stories about how the military wastes money and resources.

After I saw my first film about nuclear war and nuclear weapons, I decided I wanted to start a peace group. I had begun making connections between what was happening in my community and the cost of building all those nuclear weapons. I talked about starting a group at Quaker Meeting a couple of times, but people didn't seem to be overly interested. Then, one day a woman named Carol came into the Meeting.

We both had a vision of working for peace. I guess I was looking for someone to be the leader, and I assumed Carol would be willing to do it. But she said, "Linda, look at me. Do you think people would take me seriously as a leader?" And I looked at her wild hair and "hippie" clothes and said, thinking out loud, "No, you're not the leader we need for Charleston, South Carolina." We both knew she would not be trusted by local Charlestonians because of the way she looked and because she was not from the area. So she said, "You have to do it." It was scary to think that it really was up to me to be the leader, but I had found someone to support me, and that was all it took—one other person.

We started by putting an ad and articles in the local paper saying we wanted to start a peace group and announced that we were going to have a meeting. At the first meeting, we hooked up with Steve who was a doctor at the University of South Carolina Medical School. We planned a public meeting and showed a film about nuclear war.

I was excited about our first public meeting, but what took place was very difficult for me. At the meeting, Steve started explaining to the newcomers what our group was about and then he turned to me and said, "Linda, do you want to say something?" Lacking confidence, I said no. I didn't speak another word during that first meeting. The people were nice enough, but it was just incredibly intimidating for me, a secretary, to speak in front of this group. Instead, I volunteered to do a lot of the work before the next meeting. We continued to meet for a while in this way, and I continued to volunteer but spoke very little. Sometimes, I would give a report on the organizing, but always with great apprehension.

Many people assume that a working-class woman without a college education can't speak effectively. I found these attitudes even within the peace movement, and I accepted them as true. As our group started growing, more college-educated men came in. One new member, Ken, had been active in peace work before. Ken was a scientist. When he came into the group, he basically took over the leadership role. Although I had been too intimidated to speak up before, I had at least maintained a role in the organizing. But now, all of a sudden, even that became hard for me to do. I volunteered for the work more than ever, but I remember feeling that I was slowly becoming invisible. In a discussion about who should be the speakers in community churches for an event we had organized, I volunteered to speak because I really wanted to do more even though I felt terrified about it. Someone said, "Well, you know, I think Ken might be a better person to speak to this group because people will listen to a doctor more." I felt I wanted to crawl inside myself and disappear. Before this incident, I had been afraid to speak but I had thought I had a lot to contribute to the peace movement. Afterwards I thought I had nothing to say that anyone would want to hear. Ken, a college-educated man, a professional, was "articulate." And I was told I was inarticulate. (I heard the word "articulate" used to describe people so much in the early days of the peace movement that I learned to hate it!)

Then one day, I got a call from Steve, who was supposed to speak at a Black Ministerial Alliance meeting. He said he couldn't make the meeting and asked me to go—not to speak, but just to take materials there. So I went to the meeting, in a church chapel in the black community. After they had taken care of their business, one of the ministers stood to announce that he wanted to introduce the speaker of the day—me! Going up to the pulpit, totally unprepared, I dropped all my papers. When I said something about dropping my papers because I was so nervous, they said, "Don't be nervous . . . don't worry . . . it's fine." Of course, I didn't know what I was going to speak about. I just fumbled around for a little while, and then I started talking about my peace work and how I felt about the connection between the military budget and the poor housing in our community. I explained that I lived in this community and that I was concerned with the landlord problems and crime. I just started talking about how wrong it was that money went to the military instead of into better housing. I was speaking from my heart. When I finished, I got a standing ovation.

Thanks to this experience, I began to realize that I *could* speak effectively to people in my own community, even though middle-class people gave me the message that I was inarticulate or had nothing to say. When I was talking to the general public, I felt empowered. Eventually, I was able to bring more working-class people into the peace group and I began to take on stronger leadership roles there as well.

During the time I was helping organize the Charleston peace group I moved to another low-income community near two large housing projects. I got to know folks in the neighborhood, all of whom were black, and we began talking about problems in our community. When I asked who we should talk to about our concerns, people would tell me I should talk to a woman named Septima Clark. She lived in the community and people clearly felt she would know what we should do.

One Saturday, I walked over to Septima Clark's house and knocked on the door. She immediately invited me in to eat. Septima was eighty-five years old. She lived in a two-story house, with a yard full of flowers. The house had a porch and, once inside the front door, I noticed that the furniture was mismatched with lots of covers. It felt very comfortable. It was an older house, nothing fancy, with a lot of knickknacks around. Septima was of medium height, bent over but strong, and spoke in a clear, firm voice. When I told her of my concerns for the community, she gave me the names of people who would be interested in helping me figure out how to deal with these problems. People who had worked many years on problems in the community and had experience struggling for change.

I told Septima that I was organizing people to go to Washington to commemorate the twentieth anniversary of the 1963 March on Washington led by Dr. Martin Luther King, Jr. I explained that I wanted the group to be multiracial and not just white peace folks, and she said to me, "Well, I want to go." I was surprised because she was so old. Then she added, "You know I went to the first one?" She told me a little of her personal history, how she had been a friend of Dr. King's and an activist in the civil rights movement. She told me about organizing literacy classes or "Citizenship Schools" throughout the South that taught people, among other things, how to take the test to get the right to vote. She told me about being fired by the Charleston school board for her membership in the NAACP. I learned later that she was one of the most effective leaders in the civil rights movement, that she had worked at the Highlander Center, a nonviolence training center in Tennessee, and at the Southern Christian Leadership Conference with Martin Luther King.

Septima told me that the main weakness of the civil rights movement was its sexism. She believed that women needed to become leaders within the civil rights movement. She also taught me that confusion and disagreements were OK because they meant change was happening. If I was really upset or confused, she would say, "Good, that means you're figuring it out." I still keep in mind her words in *I Dream A World* by Brian Lanker: "I have great belief in the fact that whenever there is chaos, it creates wonderful thinking. I consider chaos a gift."

Septima sent me to speak at a black community meeting. It was in a church in our neighborhood. At first, I didn't feel uncomfortable going to the meeting because I was used to being the only white person in an all black community. But then I started wondering about what right I had as a white person to come in and tell people my concerns. The black folks at this meeting were asking themselves this same question. Some members made an effort to welcome me, but others let it be known that they resented my being there.

After the meeting I went back to Septima's house and told her that the people didn't want me there. "Well, what did you expect?" she said. "What did you think would happen? Go back to the next one." That was the first time I began to confront my own racist attitudes. What did I expect? Why should they trust me? Why should black people trust some white woman who had come to their meeting? Septima explained that I had to earn their trust.

I had believed that I was not racist because I had always believed in equality and had African American friends. I began to understand that I still had attitudes and ways of being that were racist even though I didn't mean to be. I had grown up and had been taught in a racist society. I could not escape from that even though I sincerely wanted to. I began the long struggle of trying to "unlearn" racism, a struggle which I know will take the rest of my life. But I knew that I could not let this realization stop the work I had to do. I knew that there were some black people who didn't believe whites and blacks should work together, but I also knew that as a low-income white person, the only chance in hell that I had of ever creating social change was to figure out some way to build bridges with black folks who were also oppressed. I had to find some way to earn their trust. Maybe it was because I lived in low-income communities, rode the buses, and spent most of my time with people of color that I had this consciousness. Septima Clark was the person who made me understand the painful work of building those bridges, and I will always be grateful for her lessons.

I began working in the black community where I lived and started organizing in the Charleston area for the twentieth anniversary of Martin Luther King's March on Washington. I worked at that time in the same office with a black attorney. I told him one day that I had decided that I wanted to make it possible for low-income folks to go to Washington. I asked him if he wanted to go, and he said no. I was learning some fund-raising skills then, so I said, "Will you buy a ticket for someone to go in your place?" He said, "I don't know about that, who's going?" I said, "Septima Clark is going." He said, "Oh, I'll buy a ticket for her." I went to several law offices and asked them all if they would buy a ticket for Septima Clark. I probably sold over twenty seats for Septima. The March was an incredible experience both for me and for the many young people who were able to go in one of "Septima's seats."

After the March on Washington, I went to Columbia, South Carolina, for a housing demonstration modeled on the "Hooverville" tent cities of the Great Depression. We built shacks out of cardboard and occupied a city property for a weekend to demand that more city money be allocated for housing. There in "Reaganville" I met a woman who was a full-time organizer. I asked her how she got paid to be an organizer and explained that I wanted to get that kind of job. She said that I had to raise the money and that it was very difficult. That I would have to write "proposals" and raise the money from "foundations." I didn't know what a foundation was.

I went to Friends Meeting and told folks that I wanted to become an organizer. One of the women there explained to me that I didn't have the experience to be an organizer. "Oh, Linda, you don't want to do that. You have to know how to raise money and how to manage people and speak publicly." I refused to be discouraged. I went to talk to two of the strongest activists I knew in the peace movement in Charleston about becoming an organizer with the local peace group. When they said that we didn't have the money to hire a staff person, I offered to raise it. By this time I had some experience in raising money. I organized a nuclear freeze walk-a-thon and raised enough money to support a year's salary for a full-time community organizer. When it appeared that it still wouldn't be possible for me to become a staff person of the Charleston organization, I applied for paid organizing jobs outside of Charleston. But when people in Charleston realized I was serious about leaving, they decided to offer me a job after all. I made plans to quit my secretarial job and work full time as an organizer, following my dream.

In December 1983, just a few weeks before I was to begin working as an organizer, Mama called me and told me that Daddy was feeling really bad. He had gone to the doctor, who said he had the flu. He was fifty-four years old. In 1966, he had gone to work for a textile plant and had worked there for seventeen years without ever having a vacation. He got no sick days. He was considered a "temporary" employee, which meant that we couldn't even use the employees park. He didn't get paid for holidays, so if he wanted to take Christmas off, he had to work three sixteen-hour shifts. The week before Mama called me, he had worked sixteen-hour shifts on Monday, Tuesday, and Wednesday, and on Thursday, when he came home at five, he was really sick. On Thursday evening he went back to the doctor who this time gave him a shot of penicillin and sent him home. I called that morning and talked to my father. "Daddy I'm really scared," I said. And he said, "Yeah, I am too."

I knew he was dying. I don't know how but I knew. I had been packing to go home for Christmas when Mama called, and now I packed the only two black dresses I owned. I cried all the way back to Woodleaf, and when I got to our house, no one was there. A neighbor told me my father had been transferred to Baptist Hospital in Winston Salem, and when I arrived my father was already in a coma from internal hemorrhaging and considered brain dead. We asked that they unhook him from every life support machine. The doctors said they had no idea how long he would live, that it could be days or weeks before he died. I prayed that he would live until my sister Jane got there.

My father died that day, just a few minutes after Jane and I went in to see him. I had talked to him that morning, and he was dead that evening. He had worked fifty-six hours in the four days before he died. The autopsy revealed that he suffered from a rare kind of leukemia, which I believe he got from exposure to chemicals at the plant.

The world I faced the morning after my father died was very different from the one I'd been trying to shape for myself in Charleston. I faced the fact that my disabled mother could not live by herself. In Charleston I lived in a third-floor, three-room, walk-up apartment and was about to embark on an unsure future. I didn't see how she could live with me there. My sisters both had families and were not willing to help support our mother. And so after the funeral I drove back to Charleston to pack my apartment and move back to Woodleaf to care for my mother. The money I had raised to pay my salary as a full-time organizer for the Charleston peace group would be spent to hire someone else. On Christmas day I moved back to North Carolina, back to the Piedmont, where a new chapter of my life would begin.

3

PPP: Creating Our Own
Model for Social Change

THE STORY OF the Piedmont Peace Project is the story
of people creating a new model for social change based
on the perspective of low-income and working-class
folks. It's a story of mill workers, farmers, service workers, and
others finding their voices and becoming leaders in their own
communities. It's the story of a vision—the vision I had when
I first knew I wanted to be an organizer—becoming a reality.
It's the story of going from "I" to "we" as my vision would become a shared reality built on the ideas, work, and inspiration
of the people of the Piedmont. I begin here with *my* experiences, but soon I will talk about *our* work. "We" are Denise,
Susan, George, Jesse, Joan, Laura, and Connie, Tatia, and
other PPP staff who have done the organizing work. "We" are
the folks in the communities that PPP serves. The lessons
learned during PPP's early years became the organizing principles for "our" model.

When I moved back to North Carolina in 1984, I was already thinking about how to start building a local peace and

justice group. Because of my personal experiences, I wanted to create something different, a group that honored low-income people and low-income leaders. In Charleston, I had thought I would discover the something different I was looking for by working with community organizations that worked with low-income people. I had learned a lot from that experience, but still I'd found it disempowering at times and was constantly trying to figure out what was the difference I needed. As soon as I'd moved back to North Carolina, I called the American Friends Service Committee (AFSC) in Greensboro. They offered me $600 to pay for a peace conference in my home area, which seemed a good way to start. In February of 1984 I put together a list of ministers in the area who might be sympathetic to what I wanted to do and sat down to call them.

I asked the ministers if they would play a role in organizing a conference on issues of the nuclear arms race and the military budget. The first ten I called were not interested. I finally reached one minister who said he had had very negative reactions when he had tried to do something similar in the area and in his church. He told me to forget it—that what I wanted to do was impossible. But I kept calling, and after speaking to fifty or sixty people, I found eight ministers who were willing to meet to talk about putting on some kind of program that looked at these issues. The minister who had told me to forget it called me back and said, "Well, did you ever get anything going?" I said, "Well, yes, we are going to have a meeting. Would you like to come?" So he ended up coming too. We held the first meeting in Kannapolis with ministers from about four different denominations. We made up a temporary name for our group: the "Southern Piedmont Interfaith Peacemakers." We set the conference date for early summer.

By connecting with these ministers, all of whom were white, I really hoped to meet the lay people in their churches. I wanted a diverse group of people—not just ministers—but I knew the best way to get to these folks would be through churches since we live in such a religious area (sometimes referred to as the "Buckle of the Bible Belt"). I wanted to connect with folks who were interested in peace and justice issues, so I worked to find them by doing programs within the churches. Through the networks of ministers I taught Sunday School classes, did presentations for adult education programs, and spoke to women's church groups. Slowly, I began to connect with people who had an interest in and wanted to understand more about the nuclear arms race, the military budget, U.S. military involvement in Central America, and the economic justice questions raised by the slashing of funds for social programs. One of these people was Susan Plyler, who would later become one of the first PPP staff members. Like myself, Susan had grown up in the Piedmont, the daughter of mill workers. She had been interested in peace and economic justice for years and had tried to bring discussions into her church, but she had never before had the chance to connect her beliefs with her own community. Susan came to the first conference, and as soon as we met we knew we shared a vision.

I also began to set up "house meetings" based on the Tupperware party model. After I made a presentation at a church, I would tell folks that I was interested in coming to people's homes to talk more. In their homes, I would usually show a video, talk about cuts in social programs and the increasing military budget, and give people a chance to write letters to our representatives and make commitments to future work. Many people would take the first step of writing a letter and agreeing to be part of a telephone network for lobbying. A few people made a bigger commitment to become part of a group.

While I was beginning to build this Southern Piedmont peace organization, I was also working as a paid organizer. I had learned about the Carolina Community Project, a state-wide community organizing effort, and that they had some job openings. I had applied and was hired as an organizer with a voter registration project. My job was to organize coalitions in several cities to register and to get people out to vote who had traditionally not been involved in the democratic process. Through this work, I began to meet and work with folks from the black community in my local area. Voter registration became a way to enter into the black community and begin to build connections to peace and justice issues. I went to the Black Caucus and NAACP meetings to organize coalitions to work on voter registration in the local communities. I was able to connect with individuals, mostly women, within these groups, who were willing to work together with the small group of white people that I had begun to form.

In the beginning it was difficult. Black people didn't necessarily want me there and didn't trust me as a white person. I remembered what I had learned from Septima Clark and I worked to build relationships, just going back and talking to people and going to meetings until I made connections with individuals who trusted me enough to try to work together. I think the trust was built through the sharing of our similar backgrounds and helped by the fact that I talked from the very beginning about the difficulties of trying to make a multiracial group work and acknowledged my ignorance of how to do this but also expressed my desire to work at it.

By the end of 1984, we had built a small network of white

people who were interested in issues of peace and justice, and approximately one hundred people turned out for the first public meeting that we held. I had also begun to organize a network and base in the black community. We had already begun lobbying and drawing connections between the military budget and issues of health care and housing. I began to imagine building a broader coalition in the area but felt I didn't have the necessary funding or other support.

By the middle of 1984, I was contacted by peace activists in the Boston area. They were frustrated at not being able to have an impact on peace issues at the national level. Their U.S. senators and representatives were already voting right on peace issues; they wanted to find a way to influence congresspeople whose votes could be changed. The eighth congressional district of North Carolina was on their target list. When they found out about my work through one of the national peace organizations, they called to ask me to get folks in North Carolina to lobby our senators and representatives on peace issues. I began to travel to Boston to give talks. As people there got to know me and heard about how successful our lobbying work was, a few individuals began to host fund-raising parties for our Piedmont peace group. The relationship that sprang up between us North Carolinians and the middle- and upper-income folks in the Boston suburbs would become one of the most unusual parts of our new organizing model. We developed our own approach to fund-raising, one that challenged middle-class progressive folks (and donors) on their own classism and racism.

Our new supporters in Boston encouraged me to apply for foundation funding. In November of 1984, I wrote a proposal (actually, I wrote an outline and got help writing a proposal) describing the organizing base I'd built in North Carolina and my plans to expand on it. The foundations needed a name, so I called the group the Piedmont Peace Project. Piedmont was the region we lived in, and I called it a peace project because, even though it wasn't like a traditional peace group, I defined peace to include peace and justice within our own communities. Foundations also wanted the group to have a board of directors, but I stood my ground against this requirement. It was way too early for us to have a formal board. I had decided that when we did have a board it would need to be at least two-thirds low-income and two-thirds people of color and two-thirds women. We didn't have enough active folks to make this possible. Also, our folks were still new to this work; asking them to take on the responsibility of a board member was just pushing too fast. I convinced the foundations that it was okay for us to have an informal steering committee structure. At the same time, we had a sponsor organization, Carolina Community Project, which I'd worked for previously and whose board oversaw our finances and staff. This was the beginning of an ongoing process of PPP working with foundations to clarify the ways that they can be more helpful in organizing low-income and working-class folks.

As our steering committee worked together building PPP, we brought to our folks' attention the national issues which had an effect on our area. One of these issues was military intervention in El Salvador. In those early years of PPP, one of the things we did when we were talking to folks was to carry around a little brown towel that I bought in Kannapolis village. When people started to talk about those "damn foreigners," we pulled out this towel and said, "You know, you're right. We bought this towel in the local store in Kannapolis and, you're right, it's made by a foreigner. But, you know what? That worker only makes a couple dollars a day and that worker's children are going hungry. There is no money to keep his children in school and no grievance process for protesting terrible working conditions." And we'd say, "Workers can't protest because the military would be sent in by the government to stop them from trying to get better working conditions and better pay. And the worker who made this towel works for an American textile mill that closed down here and moved to El Salvador." Then we would point out that the U.S. government was supporting the military in El Salvador for the sake of American businesses. People really understood that. In ten minutes, we could have them moving from cussing the foreigners who they believed had taken their jobs to understanding that the U.S. government was responsible for protecting U.S. investments in those countries and giving the U.S. companies tax breaks to move there. We used that towel as a way to begin to get people to see that the issue was not about working people taking each other's jobs, but it was about capitalism and the U.S. government. Then we would get people to write letters to their congresspeople asking the U.S. government not to support the government of El Salvador. We learned that it was easy for working folks to make the connections between local, national, and international issues once they got information in language that made sense to them.

Those first two years of Piedmont Peace Project were really about working in both the black and white communities and beginning to figure out ways to link the two together. It was a period of learning how to talk to low-income white folks about issues of peace and justice and finding ways to connect them in. The way that we began to reach folks—black and white—was going door to door: going out in the community and just talking to people. We would go into people's homes and ask them what issues they were concerned about. For some people it was farm issues, for some it was social security and disability cuts. For some it was problems like the lack of roads and sewer systems. We would talk about what they were concerned about, and then we would begin to talk about the U.S. military budget—about how our tax dollars were going to support unnecessary weapons while critical programs were being cut. This door-to-door work became our method of doing community outreach whenever we began organizing in a new community. Later on it also gave us a way to develop written materials using the actual words of people in our communities.

As our small nucleus of low-income people grew, we were also able to bring in middle-class people. Most of these folks came in through the churches where I spoke. Some had an interest in peace work and wanted to be a part of a group. This was new information to others, and they wanted to learn more. We began to talk to them about the broader connections between peace and justice, pointing to the problems that were going on in our community. That is how we first began to connect peace and the military budget to economic and social justice.

As our organization grew in size, we began to have more of an impact. When we started PPP, our congressman, Bill Hefner, had a zero percent voting record on peace issues and only about a 30 percent voting record on social justice issues (as rated by the Council for a Livable World and the AFL-CIO). We lobbied him from the very beginning on the issues we were concerned about—housing, health care, child care, education—and we talked to him about the military budget.

For instance, in 1985, we lobbied against severe cuts recommended to social security and disability and health care funds. We organized four different groups to visit Congressman Bill Hefner, all on the same day. The first group was the peace group. They went in and talked to Hefner about the military budget and urged him not to cut social security disability. They specifically mentioned the MX missile and recommended cutting money for it in order to fund social security and other programs. Then a group of low-income white folks that we had worked with, mostly farmers, went to Hefner's office to talk about issues they were concerned about, including social security, farm subsidies, and the military budget. They also recommended cutting funds for the MX missile. The third group that went in to see the congressman was an African American group. They talked about housing, health care, and educational opportunities for the youth in their communities and concluded by saying, "We don't want you to vote for the MX missile. Use the money to invest in our communities." Finally, in came a group of disabled folks who wanted to talk to Hefner specifically about cuts in the social security disability program. When Hefner said there wasn't enough money for this program, the group said, "Well you are voting to spend money on the MX missile, why don't you cut that?" This was the fourth time the MX missile had been criticized by voters in one day. Hefner just put his head down on the table. He couldn't believe that all these voters were complaining to him about the MX missile. When the vote to cut funds to the MX missile came up a few weeks later, Hefner, who had previously supported the missile, voted against it. As we learned to lobby in new and creative ways, Congressman Hefner began to change his voting patterns. In PPP's second year, the number of people we registered and got to vote exceeded the congressman's winning margin—and believe me, we never let him forget it. Congressman Hefner's voting record has moved to as high as 83 percent on peace issues and 98 percent on social justice issues.

We could feel early on that we were doing something new and exciting in our community. But our activities were also very threatening to traditional leaders. Because of our success, we were becoming more visible. As a result we began to encounter some frightening opposition. Some of the ministers who had been quite supportive and had let us have meetings in their churches began to be pressured by individuals in their congregations not to allow us to meet there. There was some organizing against us in the churches. Then more threatening things began to happen. At times, people would actually disrupt our meetings, and others would stand out in the parking lot writing down the license plate numbers of folks who came to our meetings. At one meeting, we sponsored a program where three Mothers of the Disappeared from Central America (Madres De Los Desaparecidos) were to speak. When they began their presentation, a man came in and started screaming that the women were communists. He told people in our audience that they had better get their names off our sign-up list. A man in the audience, who was clearly a plant, stomped up to the front of the church, grabbed our guest list, and very dramatically marked his name off. It was quite a performance. The speakers had to leave without getting to make their full presentation. They were very shaken and frightened. The experience was very intimidating and demoralizing for all of us who were present. Some people decided they could no longer participate in our group, not because they disagreed with our views, but because they were afraid of the consequences.

The trouble continued. Soon we started experiencing more difficulties in finding meeting places. The library wouldn't let us meet in the public meeting room because they said we were "too political"—even though other religious and conservative groups met there regularly. Our office was ransacked and files were stolen. A church allowed us office space, only to have to ask us to leave after intense opposition from members in the congregation. Finally we moved our office back into the trailer where I lived with my mother.

In addition to this direct opposition to the PPP organization, white folks who were PPP members experienced a lot of pressure to quit the group. Some of that pressure was direct. Employers, co-workers, and community leaders pushed them to drop out of PPP or face being ostracized or fired. Some of the pressure was indirect. Members felt their family and friends didn't approve of PPP. They worried they would no longer be welcome in their own community if they continued to support PPP.

In 1987, after a particularly violent attack against us, a lot of people left the organization. I still cannot describe this time in detail for fear of jeopardizing others. Nearly all the middle-class people who had worked with us left. That hurt a lot. For a long time their abandonment made me distrust middle-class folks. I thought they would remain committed to social change only as long as it was safe and easy. While later I would change my thinking, my distrust of middle-class supporters changed the way we did outreach and organizing for several years.

After the violence, the Piedmont Peace Project went "underground" in 1987. We did outreach only to low-income and working-class communities. We organized ónly through "word of mouth." We held no public meetings, never publicized our meeting places, and often met in different places, usually in churches. Some ministers let us meet in their churches, even though they received lots of personal opposition from church members. Others allowed us to meet as long as it was kept secret. We had informal committees that decided on the direction of our work, but we did not have a formal board of directors or membership. It was a discouraging period for PPP. In time, though, we realized we were actually building a more powerful organization while working "underground." Those who remained were even more strongly committed to the vision of PPP. We continued our door-to-door work and voter registration and education. We held leadership trainings where we talked about ourselves as low-income people and people of color being the leaders in our own communities. We continued to lobby Congressman Bill Hefner and to affect his voting record on peace and social justice issues. We began to realize that there was a positive side to all the middle-class people leaving. Their departure gave us working-class members the chance to find our own power without the kind of social barriers that I had faced in Charleston when I tried to work in middle-class groups.

During the time PPP was "underground," Susan Plyler left to go to college. In her place, we hired Jesse Wimberley, a native of Moore County who lived on the small farm his family had owned for four generations. Through Jesse, our work began to spread south to other counties into the Sandhills of North Carolina. Jesse worked out of his house, which had no phone, electricity, or running water. To set up his office, we had to install a phone and convert an answering machine to run off a truck battery.

The fall of 1988 brought PPP a chance to use the power and influence we had built over the last four years. SANE/Freeze, a national peace organization, had been focusing their primary work on the test ban treaty and the U.S. Strategic Defense Initiative, or Star Wars, as peace movement folks called it. Along with some other local groups, PPP was interested in having the national peace organization focus on cutting military spending and funding human needs.

Seventeen PPP members attended the 1988 SANE/Freeze Conference and lobbied others to support our platform. We stood together to speak in favor of our platform, saying to the conference participants that we felt a focus on funding human needs would build a broader movement that would allow us a better chance to win fights on particular weapons issues. The members of the conference voted to make our issues—cutting military spending and funding human needs—the priority issues for SANE/Freeze.

As a result of our success at the SANE/Freeze Conference, our group decided that after two years in hiding it was time for the Piedmont Peace Project to come out from underground. The connections we had made with other people in the peace movement—middle-class people—who cared about what we were doing and the difficulties we faced also encouraged us to become a visible force in our community again. Though we had lost local middle-class support, we had a strong relationship with activists in the Boston area who were now helping us raise enough funds to cover half of our annual budget. Peace movement leaders all over the country knew and respected our work.

We decided to mark the end of being underground by holding a large community event, which we scheduled for a Sunday, April 14, 1989. We invited Reverend Joseph Lowery, head of the Southern Christian Leadership Conference, to speak at our event. I was feeling proud of PPP's growth and optimistic about our future. So confident in fact that the staff and volunteers were handling this major event by themselves while I was away on a fund-raising trip. Just days before the event, however, one of our organizers discovered that the Ku Klux Klan was planning to demonstrate against us. Fearing violence, we called the local police chief who told us he would not be able to provide security for us. When Reverend Lowery's staff got the word that the Klan would be demonstrating at the event, they notified us that they didn't think Lowery should come because it would be too dangerous. I faxed Reverend Lowery saying, "If you abandon us now, just when we are trying to come out from underground—when people thought they could be a visible presence—if you step back now, it will be a disaster for us." We promised to hire Lowery a personal bodyguard and immediately set to work raising the money to pay for one. We also called the Justice Department asking for federal marshals, but the Justice Department claimed that they couldn't provide any security unless there was an "active threat of violence." So we got on the telephone to folks in the peace movement, asking them to contact their congresspeople with requests that the Justice Department provide us security. The Justice Department got so tired of hearing about us that someone in their offices called my mother on her personal phone line and told her to get me to stop having people call them because there was nothing they could do unless there was an active threat of violence. My mother conveyed their message, but we kept calling anyway. Finally, Ted Kennedy's and Ron Dellums's offices got involved and called the Justice Department. Federal marshals were sent to provide security for the PPP.

In fact, a lot of federal marshals were sent to provide security for the PPP in Kannapolis on April 14, 1989. They probably outnumbered the Klanspeople. The Justice Department even sent an undercover woman marshal to sing in the PPP Gospel Choir—which didn't quite work out the way they had intended. Most of our choir is black, and the woman marshal was white, which would have called some attention to her. What really sunk her though was her dress. The choir had decided that everybody should wear black or white. It was the Sunday after Easter, and all the women had saved their new black or white Easter dresses—hadn't worn them on Easter Sunday—for this event. That gives you an idea of how important this Sunday was for our members. Well, the undercover federal marshal showed up in a polka-dotted blue and white dress. The only thing to do was stick her behind the curtain.

The PPP had rented the auditorium of the local high school for our event, and the school permitted the Klan members to be on the school lawn, right where people attending the event had to walk by. Some wore their robes, and most carried Confederate flags and signs. I remember one of their signs. It read "April 14—James Earl Ray Day." The Klan members screamed obscenities and chanted threats. Even though the federal marshals were present, many people were frightened away—especially white folks, many of whom had spent hours helping organize the event.

Still, we did not let the Klan stop us, and our April 14 event was a big success! Reverend Lowery spoke that day about how national and international issues affect the lives of low-income people, and, especially, about the need for blacks and whites to work together. Black and white working folks, Lowery said, were so busy fighting over paper boats in the mud puddle while the fat cats were laughing and had taken the yacht and gone to Bermuda.

The PPP came out from underground stronger than ever. We had not let the Klan stop us. The head of the Southern Christian Leadership Conference was excited by and impressed with our organization. We had a unique relationship with middle-class supporters in several states, especially with our group of supporters in Boston. We were registering voters in record numbers and increasing voter turnout to 80 to 90 percent in the Cabarrus County communities where we had been organizing. We felt ready to use our power to make concrete changes in the low-income communities we served.

Two new people joined the PPP staff in the year after we came out from underground. Connie Leeper, a black woman who grew up in the mill town of Kannapolis, the daughter of mill workers, became an organizer in Cabarrus County. A single mother, Connie had worked at the Kannapolis mill for many years. And George Friday, a black woman who had grown up in the nearby milltown of Gastonia, also joined the staff. George had worked for national peace and justice organizations in Washington, D.C. She came back home to run PPP's voter registration, get-out-the-vote program.

After the PPP was visible again, one of our first major organizing campaigns took place in the Midway community in the town of Aberdeen in Moore County. Midway was typical of many communities in our area—a very small, poor black community where over 80 percent of the houses were below living standards. Midway is located in the middle of Aberdeen—we call it the hole in the doughnut—and although Aberdeen totally surrounds Midway, Midway was not considered part of the town. The town officials of Aberdeen refused to annex Midway because they said it was too poor. As a result, the people in Midway could not get city water and sewer or other services. Aberdeen would not pick up their trash, so people buried their trash in their yards or burned it. Aberdeen would not respond to their fires or their medical emergencies. People had died because the rescue squad, which was one mile away, wouldn't respond to people's calls for help from Midway.

After talking to several people in the Midway community and identifying the community leaders, PPP worked with the leaders to pull together a meeting to talk to folks about what they wanted for their community. Minnie Ray, an elderly black woman who lived in the community, worked to turn out people for the meeting. Only four or five people showed up, and everyone, including the leaders, seemed depressed about being unable to do anything. Of course people were interested in annexation and water and sewer services and upgrading their housing, but mostly people had given up on Midway. In fact, at that time, if you asked the children in Midway where they were from, they would claim another community.

The long-term goal of the Midway group was to get a community development block grant to upgrade the houses and to persuade Aberdeen to annex Midway. But we began by asking the group to set some smaller "winnable" goals. Folks decided that an intermediate step would be to get dumpsters in the community so they wouldn't have to continue to bury their trash in their yards. It took more than two months for

PPP to organize a group to go down to the town council and demand a dumpster for the Midway community. People would not go—either because they were too afraid of challenging people in power or because they felt it wouldn't make a difference. Now, our organizer knew the mayor, and he could have called and probably would have got the dumpster much quicker. But it was absolutely essential that the folks in Midway do it for themselves. Once the community got the dumpster, we had a big party to celebrate.

Once the dumpster was acquired, the whole Midway community pulled together and began a major campaign for community development block grants. Representatives from Midway and PPP made trips to Raleigh, our state capital, as well as to Washington, D.C., where we held a national press conference and visited our elected representatives. We brought to a major press conference in Washington a huge wooden missile made by peace activists in Charlotte, North Carolina, which turned into a house when you opened it. We showed how money from the military budget could be used for our community's needs. We also brought with us six-foot report cards which rated our representatives on their votes about housing which would benefit Midway as well as other communities. After we received national press coverage and were featured in a public television documentary called *The Rage for Democracy* (which aired in April 1992), other people in the surrounding communities became aware of the conditions in Midway and began to offer their support. As a result of three years of continuous organizing, folks in Midway have not only received a community development block grant which has allowed them to fix up their housing, but they have won other important victories like water and sewer services and paved roads. Midway, which is still working for annexation today, looks very different than it did three years ago.

Even more important is the fact that people in Midway found their voices during this process. Folks who led that fight are now leaders in our organization and are helping to organize in other similar communities. Now, the community leaders and the people of Midway are outspoken and proud to claim their community. Because of their victory, many surrounding communities have begun to hope for themselves and ask PPP to help them organize.

Midway is a success story, but sometimes we have learned as much from organizing campaigns where the victories were mixed with disappointments. While we were working in Midway, some community folks approached us about the Proctor-Silex Hamilton-Beach Corporation (referred to locally as just Proctor-Silex). A lot of folks in Midway worked for Proctor-Silex. The plant employed eight hundred local workers. They made small home appliances like toasters and irons. Approximately 80 percent of the workers were women. Several PPP members worked there. In the spring of 1991 Proctor-Silex announced that they would be phasing out their operation in Moore County and moving to Mexico. People were going to lose not only their jobs but also their health insurance and possibly their pensions as well. The plant would also leave behind many disabled workers who were unable to work in other jobs and was walking away from a toxic waste dump. Our members and board of directors asked the PPP staff to address these problems.

We began by organizing with our board members and members who worked at Proctor-Silex to pull together a meeting of other workers. We began that meeting by letting people speak of their concerns and fears, and then facilitated a process of getting workers to identify issues and goals. And last, we began to educate people on the issue of "maquiladoras"* because our folks were blaming the Mexicans for taking their jobs. Just as with our earlier organizing about El Salvador, it was important for folks to understand that they shouldn't blame poor people in Mexico, but instead they should criticize the U.S. corporations and government policies (tax breaks and incentives) that supported moving plants out of the United States. We talked to plant workers about the Mexican workers who were getting their jobs—mostly women who are incredibly oppressed and working in horrible conditions that are destroying their health. We knew we'd made progress when one of our members who worked at Proctor-Silex said, "Used to be when I saw a Mexican worker, I just wanted to run them down in my truck, but now I know that they're poor people, just like me, trying to feed their children."

We never really expected to stop the plant closing because we knew the process was too far along. But we wanted to win as many protections and rights for workers as we could. One of our major goals was to get retraining funds for the workers. We eventually won $500,000 to retrain the workers, but these funds went immediately to the state of North Carolina which turned over the money to a "private industries council" which had been established by the federal government. The council, which by law must be made up of over 50 percent of corporate heads and executives, directed the money to the local commu-

---

* U.S.-owned factories in Mexico that use Mexican workers to assemble goods for the U.S. and other foreign markets. The workers are often mistreated, given very low wages, and have unhealthy working conditions.

nity college to provide training for the workers. What kind of training is offered is also determined by the council. So far, the training offered has been for jobs in the region's manufacturing plants, where there are actually very few openings. Salaries for these jobs are low—as they usually are when a company expects many people to compete for only a few positions. The plant workers had hoped instead to receive training that developed new skills, opened new employment opportunities, and stimulated economic growth.

The Proctor-Silex campaign made us at PPP realize that it wasn't going to do us any good to work on local issues unless we began to address federal laws that allow funds to be diverted in this way from the people who really need them. We knew we had to work to place our own people on the federal commissions and boards where the decisions get made. We determined after the failure at Proctor-Silex to make organizing for economic democracy a centerpiece of our work.

However, in 1991 the Gulf War drastically changed our focus. By December 1990 we were convinced there would be a war in the Middle East. We were frustrated with the national peace organizations who seemed unconvinced that a war would happen and were not working on any cooperative plan to oppose it. For us at PPP, the war was more than a faraway peace issue. It was fathers and mothers, sons and daughters, sisters and brothers whose lives would be at risk. We knew the focus of our work would have to shift to opposing the war. We revised our work plan, postponed the start of the literacy program, and figured out that some of our major goals—like getting national media coverage—could still be met under our new plan. Many of our volunteers worked every evening after getting off from a long day at the textile mill. They helped make fliers, plan press conferences, produce a video, send copies of the video to peace groups around the country, and organize truck drivers to distribute our materials about the war all along the east coast. Many volunteers had family members who had joined the military as a way to get education, a job, and a way out of a community where working in the textile mill or in fast food service were most often their only options. Our folks clearly saw the need to oppose the government policy—not the troops. Earlier in 1990, PPP had won a national award for grassroots peace work. Part of the award was the services of a media consultant, whose advice had already helped us begin to think about the media in a new way and as one of the most important parts of our organizing and leadership development work. Our experience during the Gulf War proved how right we were. The voices of PPP folks were aired on hundreds of radio and TV stations and printed in newspapers across the United States from the local *Kannapolis Daily Independent* to the *New York Times*.

Although everyone at PPP was happy to see the Gulf War concluded in 1992, conflict still arose that year that for a time seemed to threaten the whole organization. By this time, the PPP board was well established with the percentages of low-income folks, people of color, and women that we had initially set. A few of our board members and PPP staff wanted to revise our mission statement to include welcoming all oppressed groups—including gays and lesbians—to PPP. Some of the men on the board objected strongly to this revision. Some also opposed the requirement that PPP steering committees be made up of at least 50 percent women. Later chapters will tell the full story of this crisis. Here I simply want to emphasize the lesson we at PPP learned from this conflict. It was what we had always known. We could not compromise when it came to opposing all forms of oppression. Organizing without confronting all oppression will lead to temporary victories and ultimate defeat.

By the end of 1992, PPP was recognized by many people as a different and important model of organizing for social change. We had learned to trust our own knowledge and experience as low-income people in organizing our communities; to link local, national, and international issues; to build new kinds of relationships between low-income and middle-class communities, including donors and foundations; to create new images of leadership; and to deal directly with all forms of oppression and how they affect us. Like most new things, our model would be questioned and criticized. The criticism would sometimes feel bad, but eventually it also made us understand more clearly the lessons we had learned.

4

Building Our Own Model

I WOULD LIKE to tell you the story of how the Piedmont Peace Project's grassroots organizing model came to be. The story isn't over yet, of course. Our model has been developing during the ten years (1985–1995) that PPP has been in existence, and is changing still.

When I described the journey that led me to decide to become an organizer, I talked about some of the negative experiences I had in the progressive movement. Those experiences helped me understand that most of the middle-class people working for social change did not speak to or for people like me and that I had to find my own voice. For the past ten years all of us working with PPP have been learning to find our own voices and to build a model for grassroots organizing that is inclusive. During that time we have met with opposition from many sources—among them progressive people and organizations. In fact, some of our most difficult struggles have been with other progressive organizations who don't agree with some of the ways we do things at PPP. I will describe some of those struggles in this and other chapters.

Before I begin that story, however, I want to acknowledge

the great contribution made by progressive movements in our country's history. Today, we are building on the courage, commitment, and compassion of social justice activists past and present. I want to honor their efforts and accomplishments and what they have taught us. I learned a great deal from progressive folks like Septima Clark in Charleston, South Carolina, that helped me when I returned to North Carolina. I learned many valuable lessons from people who trained me: Cathy Howell, Ron Charity, John Wancheck, and Si Kahn. I got a lot of encouragement from many progressive people and organizations even though they sometimes disagreed with or questioned what PPP was doing. And my vision for a grassroots organization for social justice was formed in part by what I took from other models.

Yet the most important parts of PPP's organizing model have evolved out of the experiences of the folks who make up PPP and out of the culture of our communities. We have taken pieces from other models when they worked for us, and we've discarded pieces and replaced them when we could see they were not right for us.

As we struggled to build an organization that worked for us as low-income people, we were questioned and criticized by other organizers, people working at the community and national level, and by progressive peace groups. These people were our allies, but they had been organizing according to models that dated to the 1960s and 1970s and were critical of the ways in which the PPP model differed from the older models. For the most part these differences developed because we were listening to the experiences of our selves and our community. Our progressive allies were critical simply because our efforts were new to them, but I also think that some of their criticism came from prejudices within the progressive movement—preconceptions I recognize as classism, racism, sexism, and homophobia. I saw evidence of these prejudices both in white, middle-class, single-issue progressive groups and also among the typically middle-class progressives who organize low-income people.

In the early years of PPP, as I've described, I became involved with the national peace movement. During this time, I was asked by a field organizer for a national peace group if I would speak at a fund-raising event in Boston. I said that I would, even though I was afraid. I had not spoken in front of a large group since the Black Ministerial Alliance in Charleston the two years before. I had never spoken to a middle-class and wealthy crowd, and I had never been further north than Washington, D.C.

A couple weeks after I'd been called by the field organizer, a national leader for the same peace group spoke at the University of North Carolina in Charlotte, and I went to hear him. His talk sounded very academic to me, but afterwards I found the courage to introduce myself and start a conversation. As soon as I opened my mouth, speaking in my southern drawl and working-class language, he drew back. The expression on his face said to me he was thinking, "Is this person for real?!" When I told him I was the person coming to Boston to speak at the peace group's fund-raising event (which I knew was costing guests $125 per couple), I could tell that he was thinking, "Oh my God, what have we done?" He began to tell me how to talk when I came to Boston, what I should say and how I should say it.

Well, I went straight home and called the field organizer. "I'm not coming to Boston," I said. "Y'all want a college professor." She said, "No, no, we want you, we want you, Linda." I was skeptical, but finally I agreed to go. I really wanted to see Boston.

In Boston, I practiced my speech again and again. I was to speak for ten minutes, and I was really scared. I had my speech memorized by the time I got to the event at this very fancy place right in downtown Boston on Beacon Hill. As soon as I walked in the door, the leader I had met in Charlotte came up to me. "Do you have your speech?" he said. "Well, yes," I answered. "What are you speaking about?" "I'm talking about my work." "How long is it?" "Exactly ten minutes," I said, knowing that was how long I'd been told it should be. "Oh you got to cut it!" he cried. "You got to cut it! You got to cut it in half! It can only be five minutes long." I went into total panic. I went flying over to my friend Jean, an experienced organizer, who had helped me with the speech. "He says I have to cut my speech, Jean, what do I do?" "Don't cut it," she said very calmly. "What! But he said I had to cut it." "Don't cut it," she told me again. "But what do I tell him?" "Tell the bastard you cut it," she said.

I just wanted to leave Boston. I knew the peace group leader thought I was going to embarrass the hell out of them all because I don't use perfect grammar and I speak with a southern Appalachian accent. I knew he thought I was going to get up there and make fools out of them in front of all their wealthy donors. But I didn't leave, and I didn't cut my speech. I went to the bathroom to try to calm down and stop crying.

The main speaker was ahead of me, a very tall, grim-looking, grey-haired man. I watched as he raised the microphone higher, wondering who he was and what he would say. He spoke for almost an hour. I couldn't understand most of what he was saying, so I practiced my own speech in my head, over and over again, worrying all the time. Finally it was my turn. I lowered the microphone with shaking hands, looked out at that well-dressed Boston crowd, and started to speak. Ten minutes later, they were on their feet and giving me a standing ovation. I was happy, of course, but so overwhelmed I could hardly make it back to my seat. When they finished clapping the peace group leader—the man who had told me to cut my speech—stood up to give the rap for money, but just as he began to speak the tall, grey-haired man crossed before him and walked over to me. "I am very honored to have been asked to speak with you and to be on the same platform with you," he said to me. "Oh my God! Who in the world is this man?" I thought. Afterwards, my friend Jean was so excited. "I can't believe he did that!" she said. "I can't either," I said. "I was so embarrassed." "Linda!" she said. "Don't you know who he is?" I admitted I didn't have a clue. "That's John Kenneth Galbraith," she told me, "a famous economist who used to work for John Kennedy!"

I felt hurt and angry by the way I'd been treated by the leader of the peace organization, but my experience in Boston only confirmed my belief that PPP's work to make working-class voices heard was more important than ever.

As we began to send PPP staff and leaders to national training sessions, we realized that we not only often spoke a different language at PPP, but there were also real differences between our philosophy and that of our trainers. I don't mean simply that we were low-income folks and the trainers were middle-class. I mean that we had to begin to understand different theoretical models for community organizing and to figure out what in these models was useful or would work for us. In other words, we had to begin to create our own model. I am not saying that our differences with the standard models have led to the perfect model even for us. In fact our model is constantly changing, but the reason it works is that it comes totally from a low-income perspective.

There are several ways in which the PPP model differs from many community organizing models for working with low-income folks. One difference is that the PPP model combines national and local issues. Many national and community organizers disapproved of this approach and felt it was an ineffective way to work. Peace activists, for example, argued that we should only work on disarmament issues. I would argue with them by saying that if people don't have housing, they are not worried about nuclear weapons. Their answer would be that PPP should tell people that nobody will have a house if we have a war, or they would tell me that working on other issues would weaken our organization's focus and strength.

Another difference in the PPP model is that, while many organizations work on changing public policy through national lobbying, we at PPP believe that we cannot make a difference unless we have a local base of power from which we can hold elected officials accountable. Building that base of power means connecting national issues with things that matter in people's everyday lives. A large focus of our work has been on nonpartisan voter registration and get-out-the-vote efforts. We have often registered and gotten more people to the polls than the margin of victory for our congressperson and many local officials. This is why, as I have said, we have been able to change Congressman Hefner's voting record so dramatically. It's why representatives take us very seriously when we lobby on both local and national issues.

While national organizers objected to our focus on local issues, many grassroots community organizers were wary about PPP including a peace agenda as part of our local organizing. They felt that we were being manipulative—that we were imposing our own agenda onto community folks. I disagree. The word "manipulative" implies being dishonest and unfair and trying to get people to do things they don't really want to do. But at PPP we were very up-front about what we wanted to accomplish. We wanted folks to see the connections between national military policy and local problems so that they understood how their own lives were affected. If they could see these connections, then we believed they could find their own voices to say what they thought was wrong or right about these national policies.

True, in a sense, we are imposing our own agenda. I know that when I first started PPP I was acting on my own beliefs. I was criticized for not caring about other people's needs, but I felt the opposite. I wanted more than getting streets paved and bringing water and sewers to our communities. I wanted a local grassroots organization with a national perspective. Without that, we might have a major impact on a few people or on one community, but we would never be able to change conditions generally, for everyone in the same situation. I also felt that the connections between local community organizing and military spending were undeniable. How could you make changes in any community with so much money tied up in the military?

Many training models are based on the idea that you can only organize people in their own self-interest. While I agree that this is basically true, I also believe you can educate people so that they understand how working on issues that reach beyond their own community is also in their self-interest. In most community organizing models, the organizer does not have the right to make any decisions about what projects community folks decide to undertake. The Alinsky* model, for instance, is based on empowering people to work in their own self-interest. The model is grounded in Saul Alinsky's belief that people should do what they feel is important in their own community. What that means is that social change within the local community, and not social change in the world at large, is almost always the focus. Alinsky believed that if you take care of local needs and empower people locally, social change on a national level will happen.

I don't believe that empowering people to work locally in their own self-interest will necessarily translate into national social change. First of all, people often don't understand the connections between local and national problems without education. Often people have been miseducated about why their local problems exist. For example, people blame foreigners for a lack of jobs, or poor people and people of color for violence, or welfare recipients for the national debt. Sometimes local people translate local needs into national and world issues, but not very many do this and it doesn't happen very often. Certainly, people do not make these translations so often or so quickly that national social changes which benefit them happen every day!

* Saul Alinsky (1909–72), a trained social worker, developed one of the first models for building a base of power by organizing poor people. He founded the Industrial Areas Foundation (IAF) in 1940, which organizes people in low-income and working-class neighborhoods. His approach to building power through grassroots community organizations has been highly influential. See his *Rules for Radicals* (New York: Vintage Books, 1971) and Sanford D. Horwitt's biography, *Let Them Call Me Rebel: Saul Alinsky, His Life and Legacy* (New York: Vintage Books, 1992).

I also believe it is important to include in an organizing model a commitment to counter racism and sexism—even if that is not part of the agenda of the local people. Many groups that have organized workers to oppose the North American Trade Agreement have had problems with the racist attitudes of the workers. People blame foreign workers for taking their jobs away. I believe that unless we deal with the racism of the folks we're organizing, any victories we have along the way will be short-lived. By educating people to change their attitudes, we change society for the long term. This kind of change is what sustains us when everything seems bleak and what inspires us when we have success.

Another way the PPP model differs from other models for community organizing is in our decision to set our own agenda. When I started building PPP, I was a local person working to create a community organization. The staff and core volunteers at PPP were leaders in our own community. We had an agenda and were developing a leadership model. We tried to take into account other organizing models, but when we were told again and again by people outside of our community who were training us to be organizers that our model was wrong—that "you can't do that"—we finally decided that they were wrong. We had our own agenda, and the organizing model we were shaping was right for us.

We were also criticized because we asked folks to accept the PPP mission and principles before becoming members. In 1992, when we were trying to revise our mission statement to include a welcome to all people who have been oppressed, including those discriminated against for reasons of religion or sexual preference, other organizers warned us against it. They said that we were imposing our own beliefs on our members.

We were also advised by senior organizers in the South that to take on an issue as loaded as homophobia with a low-income group such as ours (where a majority of people are fundamentalist Christian) would probably harm the organization by losing membership. At PPP we had always worked only with folks committed to our mission, which in our first years meant they had to be willing to work across race and class lines. Now the PPP staff decided that to be a truly inclusive organization we had to challenge our membership and board of directors around issues of homophobia. None of our folks had brought up gay and lesbian issues as an agenda item. But as a staff, we felt it was critical for PPP to be concerned about homophobia, especially since some of our members were making homophobic jokes and discriminatory remarks about gay men and lesbians. We discussed this problem as a staff and felt that we did not want to build an organization that was oppressive in any way. We wanted to stop the homophobia that was going on internally in our own organization. The discussion was very difficult. We talked about how the board would react if they found out we had lesbians on staff, and we decided that we would just tell them we were all lesbians—even our only male staff member. That was our strategy for dealing with the board; if they accused one person of being a lesbian, we would all "come out" even if it wasn't true. We would stand in solidarity with each other.

During our staff meeting, the facilitator asked us, what happens if you lose the organization? We all just looked at each other for the longest time, and I finally spoke up. "Well, we start over. We're not about building an organization that's going to be homophobic because this is not who we are." We had all agreed that we would support each other in our stand against homophobia, even if it meant we would all walk out of the board meeting unemployed. Several difficult board meetings followed. The PPP staff had to deal especially with what our folks had been taught in their churches, but finally the board of directors endorsed our stand against homophobia and it was added to the mission statement. We lost two board members over this issue, the only two who voted against the change. They pulled the chapter they represented out of PPP. It was very painful for us because we had spent two years of time and resources in building that chapter, and we were also sad that people we cared about felt they had to leave. But within a month, several folks came to us and asked to start a new chapter, and within six months almost all of the people from the old chapter, as well as new folks, had joined PPP.

Although I have just told the story of PPP's success in expanding our mission statement to welcome people who have been oppressed for reasons of sexual preference, I should add that I am not claiming that homophobia was truly overcome as a result. Even though I was willing to challenge the organization to take a stand against homophobia as a matter of principle, I was not able to take the next step of letting people know that I was a lesbian. I was afraid to make this admission because I knew I would be putting myself at risk of violence and would jeopardize PPP's credibility as well. My experience is shared by gays and lesbians across the country and indicates how deep homophobia goes.

While our local organizing campaigns were moving ahead in Moore County in the late 1980s, we discovered that our folks in Cabarrus County were stopping at a certain place in their growth as leaders. The Cabarrus County organizers had done great voter registration, get-out-the-vote, and lobbying work. They had stuck with PPP through our years of underground organizing and been part of the victory at the 1988 SANE/Freeze Conference. But some of our most faithful members in Cabarrus County were still reluctant to step into new leadership roles. We began to understand that their resistance resulted from their feelings about their reading and writing abilities. Many of our folks got the message in school that they could never be good readers or writers and they came to believe it. Once, I had believed the same thing about myself, but now I knew better. In late 1990 we decided to develop our own literacy program. It began as a way to empower folks who were letting their fears hold them back. It also became a place where we learned many lessons about how to confront different forms of oppression—how to talk about issues like sexual identity and religious differences in ways that changed the thinking of folks who had been taught fundamentalist Christian ideas.

Once again, we were challenged by a few organizers—this time for the way we went about our literacy program. When we started the literacy class, other organizers told us we ought to let folks choose what they wanted to read. Their model of empowerment required letting people make those kinds of decisions. We knew that many people in our community would most likely choose to read the Bible. Many elderly people in our community want to learn to read so they can read the Bible. Organizers who were consulting with us on setting up the literacy program said, "That's okay, let them learn how to read the Bible as long as it's their choice." One consultant suggested that we should teach the Bible from the perspective of Liberation Theology, an approach we had considered, but we felt unprepared to take on the large task of introducing Liberation Theology to people who were so completely brought up in the fundamentalist Christian church. Instead, we proposed that as a political organization with a specific agenda we would have folks read books about people like themselves, people struggling with poverty and other hardships who were able to find their own power and influence their surroundings.

As the Piedmont Peace Project grew, we purposely hired a multiracial staff who came from low-income and working-class backgrounds. We currently work in a twelve-county area of North Carolina, and all PPP staff come from the rural South and most from the communities that we work in. I believe it is important not only that our staff come from the communities we work in, but also that they represent the constituency that the organization is working with. This is a nontraditional approach to organizing and means that we endorse an indigenous organizer's experience and understanding of the community as significant and beneficial. Some groups were critical of us for taking this approach to hiring. They felt we should work in the traditional role of an "outside" organizer who has no agenda, but only responds to what the group wants. It may be appropriate that outside organizers be trained not to impose any agenda on the communities they organize, but as leaders from within the community become organizers, there need to be different ways of looking at the organizer's role.

Many progressive organizations have begun to understand that hiring indigenous people is critical in building for successful change, yet they are still using many of the same training techniques they used for "outside" organizers. At one time Acorn, a national group that organizes in low-income com-

munities, argued that community leaders should not be organizers.* In recent years, Acorn has changed its policy, and
many of its organizers now come from within the communities they serve. However, many of the people Acorn has hired
from within the community have had problems using the organizing model that Acorn developed for middle-class outside organizers.

These changes in attitude toward indigenous organizers,
and the difficulties they face in using traditional organizing
models, remind us of the middle-class roots of the progressive
movement in America. Inherent in them is a fundamental
flaw, an enduring classism. What am I, a low-income woman
who has struggled to overcome the feelings of powerlessness
and inferiority so common to others like me, to make of these
words from Saul Alinsky—a man famous for his heroic efforts
to organize poor and working-class people, but also a man
who claimed a background of poverty but who actually grew
up middle-class and later married into wealth:

> We are not here concerned with people who profess the demo-
> cratic faith but yearn for the dark security of dependency where
> they can be spared the burden of decisions. Reluctant to grow up,
> or incapable of doing so, they want to remain children and be
> cared for by others. Those who can, should be encouraged to
> grow; for the others, the fault lies not in the system but in them-
> selves.**

What I reject in Alinsky's words is his classism, his blame for
the victim. In doing so I renew my belief that fault does lie

---

* See Gary Delgado, *Organizing the Movement: The Roots and Growth of Acorn* (Phil-
adelphia: Temple University, 1986). Acorn, like IAF, was founded by a white, middle-
class man.

** Alinsky, *Rules for Radicals*, p. xxv.

in the system and call for different ways of looking at low-income folks and at the role of the organizer.

Sexist, classist, and racist viewpoints about who makes a good organizer are still expressed today. For instance, Ed Chambers, with the Industrial Areas Foundation, has been quoted as saying, "The best organizers we've got are stable married men."* His view is reflected by a staff which includes only one woman among eight national organizers and field supervisors, and by the IAF's board of trustees, all members of which are men.**

So far I've talked primarily about decisions we've made at the Piedmont Peace Project that affect our leadership model and the ways we approach organizing people in our community. I also want to describe the important work we have done in learning how to "build community" within our organization. After the period of major outside harassment that I've described previously, many people left our organization and PPP went underground in 1987. Internal fighting and stress which was related to outside harassment, racism, and sexism began to surface in PPP. We did not have a good way to deal with these internal problems. We did not feel safe talking to each other, and we had not built any communication skills among ourselves.

In 1989, another staff member and I began to seek counseling for our own problems in communicating with each other. The organization began to deal with racism and sexism within the staff and among membership. We also began to explore

---

* As quoted in Reitzes and Reitzes, *Alinsky Legacy—Alive and Kicking* (Greenwich, CT: JIS Press, 1987) from Leon Howell, "The Legacy of IAF," *New Conversations* (spring 1983): 23–27.

** Cynthia Perry, *Industrial Areas Foundation, Fifty Years: Organizing for Change* (American Communications Foundation, 1990).

how our own lack of self-esteem and our self-doubts were played out in ways that were racist and sexist. As the staff began to examine our own oppression and how it affected us, we were able to see clearly how these same issues influenced PPP members—and therefore affected our ability to build a strong, healthy organization.

Our first formal attempt to deal with these concerns was a staff retreat in 1991. At the retreat we made a pledge to each other to continue to work on team-building and communication by including some time for these subjects in every monthly staff meeting, and by holding an annual team-building retreat with a facilitator whom we hired to help us. We also saw that communication and team-building needed to be a priority within the entire organization, and the board agreed to make it a policy that we include a communications or team-building training at our annual board retreat and training on issues of oppression at every membership conference. This included working on issues of racism, sexism, and homophobia, as well as ongoing trainings around internalized oppression.

It takes a long time to build this kind of stable internal communication and trust. Many groups have said they would like to incorporate communications training, but that they just don't have the time and resources. In a panel discussion at the Kennedy School in 1993, I argued that the time and resources spent on this kind of training are essential to building long-term organizations, and listened to a key IAF organizer who said that doing this kind of work took too much time and reduced the number of political victories. I don't believe we can win the change we want without first building an organization whose inner workings reflect the same commitment to equality and mutual respect that we strive for in our organizing work.

One of the greatest benefits of community building within our organization is the fun that we all have together. We even sing together—we have a PPP gospel choir—and we play and celebrate together. As a result we have shared more about our differences in age and religion, and have learned from these differences. We have also been able to truly experience our cultural differences by sharing food, customs, and different ways of celebrating. We have developed family.

At our most recent annual membership conference, for instance, 25 percent of the participants were children. We had a political workshop on economic democracy as well as a workshop on gender issues. The PPP choir would sing people back to order. The literacy or study group presented a play based on historical black people who worked for social change, and we ended with a "teaching" cultural event with steel drums and dancing.

"Community building" has become a priority in all our organizing and training. I believe that it has been essential to the success of the Piedmont Peace Project. The time and resources we have spent in building a strong team and community have ensured that both PPP and the work we do for our community are successful for the long term.

At PPP we know that the model we have built—one that differs from that of many other groups—needs to constantly change and improve. We also feel that progressive organizations, both national and local, also need to make changes in order to be more inclusive and build a winning movement for social change.

5

....

Why Aren't We Winning?

D EALING WITH OPPRESSION is the most serious problem facing the progressive movement today. Classism,
racism, sexism, and homophobia—all forms of oppression—have divided us as a society and as a movement,
and kept us fighting among ourselves. Oppression in all its
forms has kept us from building broader and stronger organizations for social change and from being more successful in
reaching our goals.

At the Piedmont Peace Project, we define oppression as
prejudice plus power. Many people can be prejudiced, but
prejudice without the power of society to back it up is not, in
this definition, oppression. A lot of people say, "Well, black
folks can be racist too." In our definition of oppression, we
would say that African-Americans and other people of color
can hold racial prejudice against whites (or against other
people of color), but they cannot be racist. Prejudice is a personal feeling or belief. And a prejudiced person can discrimi-
nate on an individual level against someone from another
group. But the oppression of racism means one group (in our
society, whites) has the power to use all the institutions of the
society to enforce their prejudices against other races.

Oppression is part of the fabric of everything we do and ex-perience—what we're taught in school; what we see in the media and on billboards; the images of beauty we absorb from our culture. In school we learn about the white men who sup-posedly discovered everything and invented everything. In a majority of churches, women in the Bible are presented in negative ways; we're taught that men are supposed to have power over women. Men are always shown as the powerful ones. Heterosexual couples are always shown as the basis for a family; theirs is the only acceptable kind of love. Poor people are shown as stupid and lazy, often as Southern, so many people actually associate Southern accents with being dumb. All these images reflect institutionalized oppression.

While it is always possible to find a few exceptions—text-books that pay attention to the contributions of women and minorities; churches that offer alternative, nonsexist interpre-tations of the Bible; multicultural events sponsored by local communities—the great weight of the system operates as if the oppressive images were true instead of lies and distortions. For example, if you are poor and you want to buy a used car, you soon find out you'll have to pay more interest, make higher payments, than for a new car. So you end up having to buy a new car. People then say disapprovingly about you, "Look at that. He's driving a new car." They don't understand all the ways the system works to create false appearances. In-stitutionalized oppression is when a prejudice is supported by all the systems of society with all the power to back up that prejudice, so that it becomes the canon—the accepted way. Blacks may have a different image of "white," but they don't have the power to get that image on TV. In the United States, enough power backs those false images of oppressed groups that they acquire the force to keep people down and in their place, to keep people separated and not able to be a part of the power.

Oppression can be hurtful even to people in the oppressor group. For example, sexism can be damaging to men who are taught to deny their feelings as unmasculine. It can be especially hard on the men who try to break out of the traditional roles expected of them. However, men still benefit from the privilege of being a man in a male-dominated society. For instance, on the average they make twice as much as women do for equal work. It is important for men to deal with the way they have been damaged by growing up in a sexist society, but they should do so without denying their privilege as men. Racism is hurtful to white people, in the way that it keeps whites from being able to build community and close relationships with people of color. Also, by adopting "white" culture, many whites are denied the rich ethnic cultures they come from. Yet whites still benefit from white privilege in a racist society, from major economic and educational benefits to the fact that whites can buy "flesh"-colored bandaids and hosiery in the stores. And wealthy people are often hurt by classism in that it isolates them from others, but they benefit from access to resources and from a society that gives them preference over working-class and poor people.

Unless institutional power reinforces the hurt and prejudice suffered by a group, it is not oppression. By definition, a person of color cannot be racist, or a woman sexist, because they do not have the institutionalized power to act on their prejudices. Also, by definition, all white people are racist, not just because of the personal attitudes that we usually think of as racist, but because of the privilege white skin brings in our society. Whites cannot say they are not racist because they are born into a society that teaches racism and reinforces white privilege every day even before they can be aware of it. Whites *can* choose, however, to be active antiracists, which means making a commitment to a lifelong process of learning to recognize racism in themselves and in the institutions they are part of and taking steps to stop it. The same thing is true for men who can choose to be antisexist, middle- and upper-income folks who can choose to be anticlassist, and heterosexuals who can choose to fight homophobia.

Because we are all products of the world we live in, it is understandable that oppression is also a problem within the progressive movement. Most people involved in progressive organizations see themselves as fighting oppression that is "outside," in the larger society. We all agree that our goal is to end oppression in the world. However, what we have found is that very often it is oppression on the "inside" that keeps us from achieving our goals. Progressive people from the oppressor group carry into their organizations all the things they've been taught about the group they serve and oppressive ways of behaving toward the "other." Usually without intending it or seeing it, middle-class progressive people behave in ways that disempower low-income and working-class folks; whites do the same to people of color, men to women, and heterosexuals to gay, lesbian, and bisexual folks.

Another way oppression affects us is through what we call internalized oppression. Internalized oppression wouldn't exist without institutionalized oppression; it's a result of or symptom of institutionalized oppression. Internalized oppression is what happens to our self-image when we who are oppressed by race, class, and/or gender inequality accept the societal messages about being "less than": less smart, less deserving, less valuable. Not only do white and middle-class people grow up with racist, classist, and sexist images, but so do poor people, people of color, and women. We take these images in. We see ourselves on TV in these roles that are dumb or not smart. We never hear about people who are like us in school. Those messages are internalized, and we feel bad about ourselves. Internalized oppression leads to a lack of self-esteem, even self-hatred, and the hatred of others like us. It reinforces the silencing of low-income and working-class voices and the voices of women, people of color, and gay, lesbian, and bisexual people.

As well as silencing us, internalized oppression can also lead us to blame others who are oppressed. For instance, some poor whites blame blacks when they can't get jobs; some African-Americans blame Asians for controlling small businesses in black communities; some working-class people blame people on welfare as the cause of high taxes. Instead of looking at the larger society and those who control all the institutions, blame is placed on other oppressed groups. Often internalized oppression causes us to hate people like ourselves. Poor people who are working at poverty wages might despise people on welfare; black folks who adopt white hairstyles might criticize people who choose more natural or African-type hairstyles as "creating a bad image for all of us."

I am reminded of an incident that occurred at the Piedmont Peace Project offices when the documentary *The Rage for Democracy* was being filmed. I agreed to let the camera folks come in and tape a meeting with a group of our members during which they talked about their lives. This was not smart on my part because, had I thought about it, I would have realized that the film crew and cameras might make some people feel uncomfortable and exposed. During the filming one member started attacking the staff and other members who said anything about being poor. She called people "white trash," chastised every one of us for talking publicly about our oppression, and even told one person that her grandmother was turning over in her grave. It was clear that her own feelings of shame about her poverty led her to attack people who had the courage to speak the truth about their own poverty.

Very often, internalized oppression causes us to hate and blame ourselves. Women might feel inferior because they don't "think on their feet" and express strong opinions immediately in meetings; low-income folks might think they must be stupid because they don't understand all the references a speaker makes to things only middle-class people are likely to know. When we belong to a group that is oppressed, overcoming the internalized oppression has to be an ongoing part of our work for social justice.

I first began to understand my own internalized oppression when I went to Nicaragua in 1986, a trip that was one of the most powerful educational experiences I had ever had. In our first years, we did a lot of work at Piedmont Peace Project concerning Central America, so I wanted to go to Nicaragua. I had heard that the poor and working people there had taken over and set up their own government and were working to make economic and social justice a reality for all people. I went as part of a delegation to meet with leaders and community organizers who were active in the revolution.

Going to Nicaragua was a turning point in my life. There, people were proud of being "peasants." They didn't like the conditions they lived under and had fought a revolution to overcome them. They were a proud people and did not blame themselves for the conditions that affected their lives. They understood that class-based inequality is the most difficult problem facing the United States.

I was in Nicaragua on the sixth anniversary of the revolution. We had planned to get up early the morning of the anniversary and drive to Managua, the capital, for the celebration. At 4 A.M. the local people came out into the streets shouting and banging pans, waking everyone to go to the celebration. By 5 A.M. we were on the road to Managua. Even though it was a two-way road, traffic in both lanes was headed toward the capital. No one could leave Managua on that road on the morning of the anniversary. Everyone in the country was going to the celebration. The two lanes were divided by the "slow and slowest." We were in the left lane with all of the buses, trucks, and automobiles driving at a very slow pace. In the right lane were wagons pulled by horses and livestock and people on bikes and on foot. I had never seen so many ecstatic people. The buses and trucks were overloaded with people hanging onto the sides, riding on the hoods, and balancing on the bumpers. It was such a powerful scene that I felt tears streaming down my face. I was trying to hide my emotion from others on my bus because I was embarrassed, but when I heard someone else begin to sob, I looked up to see the whole busload of North Americans I was traveling with all crying. We were crying for all of these poor people who were so proud of themselves and their country for what they had been able to accomplish. They still did not have many resources; they were still poor, but they were very powerful and independent. There was no evidence of the feeling of shame that I had felt growing up poor.

The more I began to recognize classism and see its impact on me, the more I could recognize this internalized shame in other people. I began to have a whole different way of seeing things. Until then, I had looked at my poverty as my own fault or my family's fault. After Nicaragua, that all changed. What stayed with me the longest was seeing other people who had grown up in poverty really valuing who they were. They did not blame themselves, but understood poverty as a social problem. I brought back this knowledge that kept making me question how I thought about myself and the shame I felt about being poor. I returned with a new self-awareness and an understanding that the work I needed to do in the United States was to help poor people see how classism and racism have disempowered us and how they are connected.

I often tell the story of C. P. Ellis, a former Ku Klux Klan member, because I think it shows how classism can affect people negatively as well as help people who are oppressed connect with each other across race lines. I also like to tell his story because the way he experienced poverty feels so similar to many of my experiences. However, he chose to take his anger in a direction different from me.

Studs Terkel interviewed C. P. Ellis in Durham, North Carolina—an interview he published in *American Dreams: Lost and Found in America* (Ballantine Books, 1987). In the interview, Ellis talks about being ashamed of how his father dressed and being ashamed of how shabby he looked among the other children in school. He talks about how his father tried to get a loan and was turned down and how his family could afford only five gallons of oil at a time for their huge, 150-gallon oil drum for heat at night. He talks about working all the time and finally getting money together to buy this little service station. He worked it seven days a week, twelve hours a day, and then got sick. His wife tried to keep the service station by working it herself, but the bank foreclosed on him. He explains how he had all this anger, how he felt extreme frustration, and how he started looking around for someone to blame. He couldn't blame the system because he couldn't see it. It had to be something or somebody or some group that was visible, and that's how he was drawn into the Ku Klux Klan. The Klan was the only organization that he knew of where he could feel proud of who he was. At his initiation ceremony 250 people were applauding him. He had never had such a rewarding experience and he had never felt so good about himself in his whole life. Nowhere in mainstream society had he ever been exalted. It was out of his basic need to be accepted and to be respected that he joined the KKK and he loved being a Klansman. He talks about celebrating when Martin Luther King was killed.

Ten years after he joined the KKK, Ellis got involved on the school council. His co-chair was a black woman. They were working together, but they let it be known that they hated each other with a passion. One day, he told her that his son had been beaten up because he was working with her. And she said, "Well, my kid got beat up because I'm working with you." It was at this point that they started talking to each other and discovered their many common problems. Over time they became friends, close friends. They learned, to their mutual amazement, how they were so different and yet shared so many of the same problems. At the end of his interview with Terkel, Ellis tells about the day he decided to listen to a tape of Martin Luther King, Jr., and to try to understand what he was talking about. As he was listening, he started to cry. He says,

"You may think it's crazy for an ex-Klansman to be crying over a Martin Luther King tape, but I did."

I like to tell Ellis's story because a lot of people think low-income whites are born racist. They don't understand the role classism plays in dividing blacks and whites. Ellis's story helps people understand what often happens. Ellis tells how leaders in his community who were wealthy and well-educated would call on the Klan to do their dirty business, but how they wouldn't shake his hand or speak to him on the street. They would call the Ku Klux Klan headquarters and say, "The blacks are going to be at the City Council arguing for this and y'all need to come and do such-and-such," and generally encourage them to stand in the way of justice for black people. But when these leaders who called the Klan saw him out on the street, they wouldn't even look at him. That was when he began to understand that something was wrong. When he tried to point out to other Klan members how they were being used and how what they were doing was benefiting somebody else's interest and not their own, they got really upset at him. I often tell Ellis's powerful story to white groups to help show them whose interest is really served by race and class oppression.

At PPP we began to see that oppression didn't come only from the outside. We saw how we had taken these oppressive messages and internalized them, both as individuals and then collectively as a group. We began to incorporate into our discussions at staff meetings and retreats what we recognized as instances of internalized oppression. This became a critical part of our work. We realized that, if we could learn how to overcome our own feelings of shame and inadequacy or inferiority, we could begin to figure out how to work on these problems with our membership. We kept monthly journals as we learned to recognize the fears, or hostility, or uncertainty that resulted from internalized oppression, and after each staff meeting we discussed what we had recorded in the journals. We talked about how to deal with these feelings among ourselves. As organizers, we came to understand that we were learning from our personal struggles with internalized oppression a new way of seeing ourselves, and we began to teach that new view to our members. Seeing how connected these personal struggles were to the political changes we envision empowered us all to carry on our work in the community.

As an organization, PPP has also worked hard to resist our own disempowerment. In 1990, we filed a lawsuit against Cabarrus County and the state of North Carolina for not allowing us to register people to vote on county and state property. We were not allowed to register people to vote in the state employment office or in the county social services offices where many low-income folks were found. We knew that filing the lawsuit would provoke a lot of opposition and that the press would probably undermine us, so we decided to get a step ahead and arrange a positive press conference about why we were filing this suit before the press got hold of the story on its own.

We bought a big American flag and hung it in our office behind the table where we sat to talk about democracy and everybody having a right to vote. We explained that we were about voter education and that we were nonpartisan. So we got a wonderful front-page article in both the Concord and Kannapolis newspapers. And then, about a day or two later, there was a front-page article in the Kannapolis paper in which the North Carolina state attorney accused us of lying.

The state attorney's office said that we had never even contacted the North Carolina Employment Security Commission and that they were considering countersuing us for a frivolous lawsuit. They said that, of course, they would allow us to register people to vote in public offices, that it was a right protected by state law.

The reporters who wrote this second story had been given copies of our letter making a formal complaint against the local state employment office who had stopped us from registering people to vote. When we were told by that local office that we had to get permission from the state, we wrote to the North Carolina Employment Security Commission, and they wrote us back telling us we could not register people to vote in a state office. We had provided copies of our letter and the Employment Security Commission's letter to the reporters at our press conference. So the media knew they were not telling the whole truth when they printed the story quoting the state attorney. But even more troubling was how our members responded to the newspaper article that accused us of lying. The minute the press called us liars, our members believed it. They felt that if the newspaper printed the state's accusation, then it must be true. This incident made me realize how vulnerable we were and how easily people could be silenced. I worried that this incident might destroy our whole membership base in the Kannapolis-Concord area because of the way people so readily fell in line on the side of authority.

To counter the reaction of our membership, we held a meeting where we asked people if they could recall a time when they had had any dealings with the news media and to talk about those experiences. Almost everyone could remember experiences where the media had inaccurately reported something they had been involved with. We also pulled old clippings from the Kannapolis and Concord newspapers from the 1960s that talked about the civil rights movement. Most of these articles had a very negative slant toward blacks fighting for their rights. By reminding members that the media can be biased and inaccurate, we prepared the way for a discussion about why we were always so ready to believe what the newspaper said about us and to feel guilty or bad about ourselves. The result of this discussion was a plan to address the lies that had been told about us.

We wrote a press release stating that although many inaccurate stories were being told, the truth was that we had contacted the Employment Security Commission and that we had been denied a right guaranteed us by state law to register people to vote. We stated that the newspapers had had this information and did not report it, and we asked everyone to question why the press hadn't told the full story. On the back of the press release, we included copies of our letter to the state as well as their response denying us access to on-site registration. We enclosed this press release with a letter to the local ministries, sealed them both in envelopes from an express mail service, and slid them under the church doors, figuring people would open them because they were in express mail envelopes. And it worked. Ministers read the press release on Sunday morning to their congregations, and it was very powerful for our members to hear this letter read publicly in their churches. Very quickly, we got our membership involved in helping to pass the letter out to local businesses. Within days, a reporter at the newspaper in Kannapolis called to ask us what we were we passing out. I said, "Oh, we're just putting out the truth about what happened." He asked what we wanted the newspaper to do. I said, "Oh, nothing, we're putting out our own press release, and by the time we're finished more people will have read it than read your newspaper." So he said, "Well, do you want us to print the story or not?" And I said, "Of course I do." They printed an article based almost word for word on our press release, except of course they left out the part about the newspaper not telling the truth.

The Proctor-Silex campaign in 1990 forced us at PPP to confront our internalized sexism. When we began organizing we assumed that the women who worked at Proctor-Silex would lead this fight since a majority of those who were being laid off were women. Some of the male employees who were active in that campaign, and who were members of PPP, felt that they could just tell the women at Proctor-Silex what to do. And the women accepted that! Even though they would get angry about it at times, the reality was they accepted the men's lead and let them speak for the group. When we organized a community program, one of the men arranged for the town's most prominent white men to speak for the group. They were completely willing to reinforce the authority of men who were public officials. This is how internalized oppression works; people who had just been laid off from their jobs still believed the men in power were working for their best interest. What we learned from this experience was that we had not done the preparation work regarding classism and sexism with our membership—work we now know to be essential for any organizing campaign. Even though we won victories in that campaign, we learned a lot about how we could have handled it better.

Another lesson we had to learn about oppression and internalized oppression is that we must pay attention to how different types of oppression—classism, racism, sexism, and homophobia—are interconnected, and how just about all of us, no matter how oppressed we might be, can sometimes be part of the oppressor group.

I mentioned earlier our struggle over revising our mission statement to include language about sexual preference. This was a clear example of people who have suffered from classist and racist oppression being the same people who did not want to take a stand against homophobia. The wonderful thing about that experience was seeing the change in thinking that happened for most of our board members as we talked honestly about where our beliefs about sexual preference come from. Many of our folks' ideas about homosexuality came from what they were taught in church. Religion is very important in their lives, and it took a lot of courage for them to question beliefs that were tied to their faith. Yet everyone but the two men who left came to agree that our mission statement should say clearly that we welcome people who have been oppressed in any way, including for sexual preference. Another interesting part of this story is that these two men were the same two who also objected to PPP's chapter guidelines which say that at least 50 percent of steering committee members must be women.

Even though I began to recognize racism when I was very young, it's been an ongoing process for me to see all the ways that I benefit from white privilege. I think it can be harder sometimes for poor white people to see the privileges they have from being white since they suffer some of the same discrimination because of classism that people of color suffer because of racism. For instance, my teachers had low expectations of me just like they did of the black students in school.

I've learned over the years to recognize a lot of white privilege, but there's a lot of it I still don't see. And I'm always getting surprised by it. So I would define myself as a racist who works constantly against racism. I work against racism, but I still benefit from those privileges that come from having white skin.

One experience that helps me recognize my white privilege is driving with one of the African-American PPP folks in my car. If I go to Moore County with George Friday, who's black, I know I'm going to be treated differently than when I'm by myself or with Jesse, who is white. When I'm with George, I'm aware of this difference, but most of the time when I'm by myself, I don't think about it. Being welcomed, smiled at, waited on immediately, willingly served feels "normal." When I'm treated differently because I'm with someone who's African-American, I think, "This is crazy—abnormal." But in fact it's George's normal reality all the time.

I also recognize privilege from the other side, through the experience of starting to talk and immediately seeing people react to me differently because of the way I talk. They don't have the same expectations once I speak; it changes their image of me. I used to think people's reactions to me had to do with my weight. But when I lost weight, the negative reactions didn't change. It was the way I talk. I have a heavy Southern accent; I don't talk in a way that most formally educated people talk. The way I choose my words is different. So I notice privilege—class privilege—from the point of view of someone people look down on.

Another example is having to deal with things like Medicare, where you are really treated like trash. If you're poor you are often treated badly when you need assistance. Maybe this experience is more shocking for white folks because they haven't had to deal with racism. So when white people who haven't grown up with extreme poverty have to get assistance for the first time, they can be very shocked at how badly they're treated. I grew up with it all my life, so when someone is shocked at this I want to say, "Well, big deal! I had this happen all my life, and you're shocked." It makes me think about how African-American folks must feel when a white person notices a racist act and says, "I can't believe they treated us this way." I can imagine them thinking, "Where have you been? I've put up with this every day of my life." And I've done that—been horrified at how George and I have been treated at a restaurant or in a store. I've also felt disgusted when I've heard others express shock at how poor people are treated. My response is to roll my eyes and cry, "Give me a break!"

Lessons like these moved PPP into more and more work on internalized oppression and the connections between different kinds of oppression. As we carried out this work, it became even clearer how important it was. Our experiences with the controversy over the mission statement, the Proctor-Silex campaign, the bad press over our proposed suit against the state of North Carolina, the reaction of some of our members to being filmed for *The Rage for Democracy*, and other situations showed us that failing to deal with internalized oppression and our own ability to oppress other groups could have hurt our organization. Now, before we even go into a community or take on a new project, we begin to deal with oppression and internalized oppression up front. We talk to folks in the community about how our own oppression can destroy us as a mobilized force moving toward social change. We present our mission statement that addresses issues of sexism, racism, classism, and homophobia, and we ask folks, "Do you understand what all that means? Do you understand what is being talked about here?" We have full discussions and only then do we go forward with the work.

We include some kind of training on oppression and internalized oppression at every gathering, at every board meeting, at every conference. We talk about what kinds of things interfere with our organizing work, and how best to communicate with each other in an honest and safe way. We have developed guidelines for talking to each other. For example, no one can criticize someone else's work without offering a recommendation. We try to use only "I" statements. And we remind people by putting our guidelines down on paper and creating new ones for each group before every meeting.

We didn't start out being totally honest with each other. But it gets easier and easier. It doesn't mean struggles go away. We are constantly getting upset with one another, but we have an open and honest way of dealing with those struggles now. We admit that this is not the easiest way to work—the easiest would be to ignore problems and let people leave when it gets hard to face these issues. That's not the way we've chosen to do our work. Unless we learn to communicate and learn to work with each other, we cannot build a strong and diverse progressive movement. When we've done all we can to communicate and work through issues, as we did with the homophobia we discovered when we discussed changing our mission statement, then we *are* willing to let people leave if they are not ready to take a stand together against *all* oppressions.

We are convinced that the time and energy that goes into this way of organizing is more than worth the effort—that it's the only way we will build the power to make real change.

Shortly after our struggles over our mission statement, a contractor came to the door of one of our members in Midway. The contractor was involved in the rehab work that came out of PPP helping Broadway win a community development block grant. He said to our member, "You know that Piedmont Peace Project has homosexuals in their group." She answered him, "That's right. We work together with all folks who want the same things we want." The wedge of homophobia could no longer be used to divide us.

Some organizers have commented that our process is too slow and that it takes too many resources. They assume that people will become empowered through organizing campaigns. That can happen, but when there are external attacks on the organization, people will more often than not turn on one another. I have seen this happen over and over again. Internal fighting is a major problem among political activists working for social change. It is a primary reason why so many organizations get stuck and move forward very slowly, if at all.

6

Principles for a
New Organizing Model

THE PIEDMONT PEACE PROJECT has been up and running now for more than a decade. In earlier chapters I've described some of our victories and losses, and told the story of how PPP struggled to find its true shape and voice. Here I want to speak about some of the important lessons I've learned in my years of working in PPP and looking at other models for social change. I have defined a set of seven principles that I think are essential for organizing a successful and inclusive grassroots movement.

Principle 1: Focus on social change.

Many people and organizations *confuse social service with social change.* Too often, people try to deal with whatever problem is at hand with "bandaids," by treating the symptoms of social problems rather than the causes. It's very tempting for activists to do this, especially women, because women, generally speaking, are conditioned to respond to whatever emergency is happening at the moment—to fix it quickly with whatever is within reach—rather than stop and look at the bigger picture. As Kip Tiernan of Rosie's Place, a women's shelter in Boston, tells it, women are so busy trying to pull the babies that are drowning out of the river that they never stop to go to the head of the river to see who's throwing them in.

People often think social service—giving poor people things to help them out—is all that is needed to fix things. This kind of service is important, but it falls short of changing the systemic oppression that is the root of the problem. Social service is not the same as organizing people for social change. Providing services does not result in social change. When I start talking about the work PPP does, many middle-class people eagerly tell me, "Oh, I work for the homeless" or "I give to hunger." They think social service work is the same thing as organizing. And many people think that giving money to social service organizations is the same thing as giving money to social change organizations. It's not. In fact, it's the difference between helping poor people by giving them money or giving poor people the power to help themselves and believing that they are capable of helping themselves.

At Piedmont Peace Project we do not provide social services. We work to help people understand that *they* can bring about change if they are organized. *They* can get the services they need. If we stopped being a "social change" organization and started providing for needs that people in our community have, like housing or other services, then the relationship between us and the community would change. The power dynamic would change between those who were receiving services and those who were in the position to give. It would no longer be an equal relationship.

Our literacy program is a good example of the power dynamic PPP works to preserve. At first, we thought of literacy as a social service and, for a long time, we stayed away from teaching literacy skills. But later we realized we could use literacy to empower people politically. For example, our "How to Vote" flyer was written by our members to give step-by-step instructions on everything from your right to request assistance to get to the polls to what to expect when you arrive— like having to give your name and address to a stranger (who is almost always white). Another way our literacy materials have empowered people politically is by helping them develop critical thinking skills and getting them involved in the political process. I am thinking of a brochure we developed on how small farmers were being pushed out by large corporations. Reading this brochure and discussing it moved our membership to work against NAFTA. I am also thinking of a group of mothers in Moore County. Officials in Moore County refused to fund a Head Start program because running water was not available there. When the mothers got tired of hearing this excuse, PPP helped them put together a flyer, organize their neighbors who turned up the heat, and win support for a community development block grant that included money for water lines for a Head Start center.

Principle 2: Work across race and class lines.

In the early days of PPP, we realized that no one group can win by itself. We've also seen that low-income folks have the same basic needs, regardless of race.

Unless we are willing to organize across race and class lines, we will not have the numbers and the power needed to make truly effective changes in the United States. Many movements have proven this to be true. The women's movement, for example, has not been as successful as it could be because it has been primarily middle-class and white. If women of color and low-income women were also to become active in the women's movement, there's no stopping what women could do in this country. Before that can happen, each person must be able to see herself or himself as contributing equally to the movement. A group that is made up primarily of college-educated, middle- and upper-class members has to understand that those members must work *on an equal basis* with low-income people who are less "formally" educated, but who bring different skills and intelligence to the group, before the group can expand beyond class lines. We must overcome class and race barriers in order to gain the full value of what each member has to offer.

As low-income people, we bring to our organization a clear understanding of how to talk to other working-class people like ourselves. We bring an ability to make clear connections between local and national issues. That comes out of our life experiences. Many middle-class people often assume that the people at PPP are "exceptions"—that we have skills and intelligence that are above those of most low-income people. Middle-class organizers who went door-to-door with us in our local community were surprised to discover that folks in our area paid close attention to national issues. When we asked them what they thought was the biggest issue facing our country today, many of these low-income folks said that military spending and government waste were the cause of our local problems. We didn't have to explain the connection to them. They had already made the link, while many middle-class people miss those connections. Low-income people understand that spending decisions of the government affect their lives directly because they experience it on a day-to-day basis. In fact, *they know, even though they don't always know that they know.*

Most organizations know that working across race and class lines is the "right" thing to do, but they don't put their full energy and resources into bridging these divides because they are focused on winning organizational goals. However, I'm saying that keeping the focus on reaching across race and class lines is the *only* way to win the goals. Unless we use the skills and experiences of people from all races and classes, we will never mobilize enough people to create lasting social change.

Principle 3: Include indigenous organizers and leaders.

As I've said, Piedmont Peace Project requires that the board of directors have at least two-thirds low-income people, people of color, and women—all of whom must come from the community served by the chapter. Also, three-quarters of our staff come from low-income backgrounds and from the communities we represent. There is no doubt in my mind that we have succeeded because we have honored this principle of working through indigenous organizers and leaders. I don't mean a middle-class person can never work in a low-income community or vice versa. Middle-class people have worked with us as organizers, but the people who have insured our success are the local low-income and working-class people who have worked with PPP. They understand the local folks and serve as interpreters between the different classes. An example best tells the story. During the Proctor-Silex campaign an intern from Harvard University worked for PPP doing research. He was able to use his skills and abilities in research to provide important information to us on how decisions were made about economic development and who were the people in power that we needed to challenge. Also, because he was white, male, and a Harvard student, he was able to obtain critical information from local public offices that our members would not have been able to get. His work played a critical role in the success of the campaign. However, his research and his access to government offices would have come to nothing without the leadership of workers from Proctor-Silex. Without their ability to talk to other workers and people in their community, and win their trust, our intern's research would have been meaningless.

Principle 4: Encourage diversity with ongoing outreach and training.

I want to emphasize the word "ongoing" in describing this principle. Because of our commitment to the importance of ongoing diversity work, we at PPP refuse to offer training on oppression (racism, sexism, classism, heterosexism) unless a group makes a minimum three-year commitment to at least twelve training sessions. In fact, we don't think diversity training should ever end. Certainly, it hasn't at PPP. We continuously include diversity issues in our staff meetings and retreats, and in our annual membership meetings. At these meetings, our time is divided between current organizing projects and working on diversity issues and communication skills. For instance, at our 1995 annual membership conference, morning workshops were devoted to understanding racism, sexism, and homophobia, while the afternoon workshops focused on economic development and on improving organizing skills. I believe that no organizing group will achieve long-term success unless it makes an ongoing commitment to learn how we all participate in a social system that sets us against one another, and how women, people of color, and low-income folks have all been conditioned by this system to give up their power.

Principle 5: Focus on the connections between local and national issues.

When I say that successful organizing honors this fifth principle, I am asking groups to do two things. First, I'm asking groups to educate themselves to see how economic justice, peace, environmental, and women's issues are interconnected. Many groups believe that working on single issues is the way to be most effective, and certainly many single-issue groups have been effective in this country over the short term. But, if all the single-issue groups were working together, the progressive movement would be such a giant coalition that this country would be forced to change. Now even the way we get funding is set up to keep groups apart. Foundations should be looking at how groups in the social change movement could work together and they should encourage that cooperation with their giving. If foundations and donors gave to groups that make the connections between national and local issues, we would have a much more powerful movement in this country.

Second, I'm asking organizers to welcome the work it takes to translate national issues into the local language. At PPP, we often have to seek out information to educate ourselves. We might hear from the peace community that we've got to work against this missile or that weapon system, and we have to go looking for the information that links this national issue to the immediate lives of our members. To do this, we may have to call up other groups to ask specifically about local issues of housing or healthcare. Then we make the connections between the military budget and how it affects our folks. We don't start lobbying until we figure out the local connections.

Making these connections means having people who provide different levels of information. For instance, I don't struggle to read complex documents that come from government or research organizations. Other national organizations have folks who do that and they pass their interpretations on to us. These interpretations are still at a very college-educated level, but we use them to understand how to translate the information into the language of low-income people.

One of the benefits of learning how to make these translations is that you may stumble upon an educational message that crosses class lines in both directions. For example, during the 1990 Gulf War, it was the job of two PPP staff people to try to understand the more complex issues being written about in the peace movement and to translate these issues into a language that the rest of us could understand. We had plenty of written materials on hand, but we still ended up calling people who were considered experts in the peace community to talk us through them. When we fully understood the issues, we made a video in our own language to use in our area. We were surprised to see this video, specifically created by and for low-income folks, become an important educational tool in the middle-class peace community. Eventually, over three hundred copies were used across the country in house meetings, peace groups, and schools. It was even picked up by a national satellite network. There is no question that the reason our video had an impact on others was because the people featured in it—our members—all had family and friends serving in the military, and they were taking a stand against the war. Their voices—the voices of people with loved ones at risk—gave folks in the peace movement a different and very important perspective.

Principle 6: Develop and maintain personal empowerment while working for organizational power.

Much of the theory in organizing suggests that the way individuals become empowered is by building power through the organization. While I do think that happens, it is also true that *if individuals don't have a secure sense of their own personal power, the power they gain through the organization will not hold up under pressure or opposition.*

We work hard at PPP to help people to understand themselves and their experience in new ways. First, we listen, really listen, to what our members say about themselves and about the ways they feel disempowered. For example, when we first went out into the community, one of the questions we used to ask people was what would they like to change in our society. People could not answer that question. Their response was, "Who? Me? What do you mean?" So then we changed the question to, "If you were the president of the United States, what would you change? What would you do differently?" Then people would laugh and answer the question. They could not imagine themselves having the power to make changes unless they imagined themselves in a position of power. We've asked this reformulated question to disempowered groups in different places in the country, and we always get good responses. When one of our trainers traveled to Hungary to train organizers who were working with Gypsies, he found that the organizers could not get people to talk about change. So he put the question to them this way: "If you were the mayor of the village, what would you change?" And they answered right away listing what they thought should be changed. He was struck by how communication problems for Gypsies in Hungary were so similar to problems we'd run up against in Kannapolis, North Carolina.

In working on building personal empowerment, we have also learned that low-income people are not used to having options. In the past, for example, we were often frustrated by our members' inability to come up with ideas for a membership conference. If the staff threw something out as a possibility, people would say "Oh, yeah, that sounds great." No matter what kind of option we threw out, people would immediately accept it. However, if we didn't present options, people seemed totally in the dark. It became clear that they did not know how to respond to a general request for alternatives. From this experience we developed the rule that we had to present two or three alternative options for our members to consider. We would say, "Now here are some ways to think about it; here are some possible ideas." This gave people the opportunity to consider the options on their own, and often they would discuss which idea they liked best. Sometimes they would change the options by adding to or combining the ones we had suggested. In this way, we helped people understand, first, that they had options, and second, that they could consider the options and make choices. They were not expected to accept whatever was offered first.

Sometimes, when we did door-to-door work, people would only give us limited information. When we asked what the biggest problem in the community was, people would very often say "drugs." We assumed that people wanted PPP to organize for more police protection against drug users. But then we decided that rather than make assumptions about what people meant, we needed to go back and ask them, "What do *you* think we ought to do about the drug problem?" The most frequent answer was that people in the community wanted more recreation resources for their children. Their response was exciting to hear because we realized that we could help them organize to address their needs.

It is possible to help low-income people gain a sense of personal empowerment if you listen carefully to them, help them look at their options, and help them see themselves in a position of power. All of these approaches have helped PPP build an organization of self-respecting, dedicated, and courageous members. Had PPP not made this kind of commitment to building our members' personal sense of power we surely would have lost more members than we gained over the years, lost them when press coverage made them look bad, or ugly prejudices were stirred up among them, or their families and friends disapproved of their membership, or they feared to lose their jobs or were threatened with violence. An organization cannot weather opposition of this kind for long unless its members believe in their own personal power to overcome it.

Principle 7: Be flexible and ready to create new models to adapt to needs and leadership styles of participants.

As I've said, at PPP our model is a constantly changing one. These principles are merely a point of departure. There is no blueprint for fully guaranteed successful organizing. We must always watch to see what works in our own communities. We begin with these principles, but as we begin to organize, circumstances shift and change the way we carry out these principles. There is no one right way.

One of the most important components of our model is evaluation on an ongoing basis. We must always be asking what's working and what's not. We have to be adaptable and develop new ways of measuring victories. *We must be open to new ideas as we bring more and more people into the organization, and be willing to find ways to accommodate their ideas.* The most important piece of the PPP model is that it is not a "hard and fast" model. In every community, it's going to change a little and hopefully get better. We're always changing as folks begin to think about things differently and find their voices to say "Listen."

7

Invisible Walls

W HY HAVEN'T WE YET learned to build more effective multiracial, multiclass organizations in the
United States? We'll begin to find some answers if
we look closely at the invisible walls, or *barriers*, that low-
income people and people of color often encounter when
joining primarily middle-class and white organizations.

At Piedmont Peace Project, the most consistent problem
for us in dealing with other progressive groups has been overcoming prejudice based on class. In this chapter, I want to focus on helping folks see what the barriers created by classism
look like. At the same time, I will be talking about the barriers
people encounter because of their race and, at times, gender
and sexual orientation. Confronting "invisible walls" thrown
up by race, gender, and sexual orientation is just as painful as
slamming into the ones erected by classism. We need to pay
attention to all the invisible barriers that hinder our work for
social change.

The wall of language.

When I first began my work with PPP, I often heard middle-
class people talk about wanting to include low-income people

and people of color in their groups and organizations. At PPP, we used to call this "just talk," talk that acknowledged the importance of diversity but was never put into practice. We thought if people really wanted to include us, they would act differently. They would include us in discussions, listen to our suggestions, give us responsibilities. It seemed all I heard from middle-class organizers was more "just talk," but then I began to see things differently. Because of my involvement with the team of folks in Boston who work with PPP, I started to realize that these people did want to be inclusive, but they just didn't know how.

The first step in bridging the class barriers that keep us apart is to respect each other's languages. Language creates probably the biggest barrier to building an inclusive movement, and overcoming this barrier is absolutely critical to success in organizing. I am not talking about a foreign language, but the language we use to communicate every day. I often say I speak two languages: one I use in my own community and family, and one I have had to learn in order to communicate with more formally educated middle-class people. In a sense, I have had to become "bi-lingual" in order to be accepted in a middle-class world. Unfortunately, my first language—the English I learned to speak as a southern, low-income woman—is not seen as "equal." If I talk the way that comes most naturally to me, people judge me as being unintelligent *or at least* inarticulate. We must begin to honor each other's languages and accept different voices if we are going to build a winning movement.

I learned very early in my work at PPP how middle-class people judged low-income people's language. When we were in the process of creating an educational pamphlet about child care, one of the quotes we used was a child saying, "Something has got to be wrong when the government spends so much money on the military and nothing on me." We sent it to the person doing the layout, and she "corrected" the sentence to say, "I don't understand why the government spends so much money on the military and nothing on me." A very simple change, and, for many people, it would have no difference in meaning. But it created a major difference in meaning for members in our community. When local members saw it, they said, "What do you mean we don't *understand*? Of course we understand! Do you think we're stupid or something?" That was their reaction to the different ways of using words. They did understand, and they understood that something was wrong, which is what the original quote said.

People often assume that because someone speaks differently or doesn't use correct English (by the formally educated standard), they aren't smart and are unable to make an effective presentation. Clearly this is not true, but people's prejudice against different ways of speaking often stops many potential leaders who could especially reach out to a different constituency like themselves. My own experience of feeling so disempowered while I was still clearly able to connect with people who shared my background became the basis for PPP's later commitment to redefining leadership.

I realized early on that PPP's ideas about organizing were coming up against a lot of resistance from other organizers and that this was going to be a source of struggle for me. Part of this struggle has to do with class differences, the most difficult being the different languages of class. I remember getting frustrated with words like "strategies and tactics" and feeling annoyed when other organizers talked about "negotiating terms."

I was told in trainings that "strategies and tactics" were my strength, but I didn't even understand what the words meant. Even though I had a lot of trouble with it, I came to terms with the language problem by translating what I was taught into my own language. For "strategy," I thought, oh, this is what I call a "plan." I realized that I had different words for the same concepts and that, in fact, some of the things I was doing as a community organizer, and which felt to me like just common sense, were being taught as complicated concepts.

Once I realized this, I started thinking about how I could change the language to teach other working-class and low-income people. One thing I decided I would do is always explain the language commonly used in organizing. I understood that as working-class folks started coming into the movement, they were going to hear this complex terminology and it would sound scary to them. So I decided to "translate" the terminology into low-income folk's language as I was doing organizing and training. Our PPP training program continues to make these translations now. For instance, as we began educating and organizing folks in our communities about economic development, we created a "People's Dictionary of Economic Development" that defined the difficult terms in our common language. For instance, we defined "unemployment rate" as "a government-created statistic that shows the number of people who are receiving unemployment benefits until their maximum time limit is up. Then they are dropped from the unemployment rate even if they haven't found a job. Therefore, the number of people who are actually not working is much bigger than the unemployment rate talked about by the government." And here is our definition of "underemployment": "Persons working in jobs below their qualifications or skill level and persons forced to work part-time. For example, a skilled laborer with many years' experience who has lost his or her job to a plant closing now working part-time for minimum wage at a fast-food restaurant."

While I think most people can understand working-class language (even if they don't honor it), low-income and less formally educated folks have a very difficult time understanding what I call academic language. The progressive movements in this country tend to speak only to college-educated folks. Most organizers in U.S. progressive organizations are college educated and aren't aware that they speak in ways that not only do not communicate to, but also disempower, low-income folks.

One of the people I met while PPP was underground was Randall Forsberg, who was the spokesperson and founder of the Nuclear Freeze Campaign. She ran a research organization called the Institute for Defense and Disarmament Studies (IDDS) in the Boston area. I first saw her on the plane when we were on our way to a SANE/Freeze conference in Cleveland, Ohio, in the fall of 1987. She was sitting four rows behind me on the plane, and I sat awhile trying to figure out a way to go back there and start a conversation with her. Suddenly, I heard someone asking if she could sit in the seat beside me and looked up to find Randall Forsberg in the aisle. As soon as we began to talk I realized I would have no difficulty telling her about my desire to see the peace community develop materials that low-income people could use. I explained that most organizations relied on educational materials written using the language of the college educated. She suggested that we get third-graders to help write the materials. So I had to explain that wouldn't work for adults because they have a whole lifetime of experience and knowledge. She also said that it had always been her feeling that it was the responsibility of middle-class people to do peace work for low-income people because they were too busy trying to survive. I explained to her that was *absolutely* not the issue. That, in fact, low-income people wanted to work on these issues but they didn't always know how to and they didn't have access to the language to find out how. Randy Forsberg was the first person who I felt really listened to me about the need for different educational materials. She turned to me on the plane and said, "Why don't you create the materials yourself?" It was a radical idea for me. Why had I never thought of that? Why were we always looking to middle-class people to do it for us? I decided, of course, that we have to do it, and when I said, "But we don't have the money," she said, "Let me see what I can do to help."

On that flight to Cleveland, Randy Forsberg and I also talked about alternative defense, which means ways to keep this country safe without sending military forces everywhere and without using nuclear weapons. I said that we talked about that all the time at home, except that we just called it "real defense." At PPP, we didn't take the stand that we had to get rid of all military weapons. We knew we could not use that language in our community and get people to listen to us. So what we said to local folks was, "Let's talk about a *real* defense, and ask what is *real* security?" We would explain that real defense is not building more and more unnecessary nuclear weapons, when we already have enough to destroy the world several times over, but instead it's using some of the money being wasted by military spending to create a secure plan for small farmers to keep their farms, and to fund job training, education, and other social programs.

As a result of our conversation, Randy Forsberg asked me to work on a committee that would explore ways to talk about alternative defense to peace movement folks. I thought that was a very exciting idea: turning technical language into an average person's language. After the SANE/Freeze conference, she provided me with all of the technical language I needed to write a proposal to a foundation she advised which funded work on alternative defense. I knew that alternative defense was exactly what we were talking about in our work at PPP, but when I tried to write a proposal using technical language, I went crazy. I spent a week on the proposal, usually in tears. So finally, I just ripped it up and rewrote the whole proposal in my own language. I wrote a cover note saying that we're always asked to use technical language, but that frankly this is not the way we talk about alternative defense. If we did talk about alternative defense using this language, we wouldn't get any response in our community. "I'm sorry," I wrote, "but if using this language is a requirement to get the funding then we can't get it." I sent my proposal with that kind of letter, and we got funded. It was the biggest grant we'd gotten at the time—$20,000. From then on, I knew we had to use our own language when writing proposals, and that we should view the experience as an opportunity to build an honest and trusting relationship with foundations.

Recognizing and honoring working-class language is important even for low-income people who have learned to be bilingual. As anyone who has traveled in a foreign country knows, *when you are speaking in a language outside of your own, it is much harder to communicate. It is a barrier to feeling powerful.* When I am having trouble translating what I want to say into language that is acceptable to another person, I have a much harder time speaking powerfully and with self-assurance. Instead, I am unsure of what I'm saying and much less able to speak clearly about what I know. I remind myself that, even though it's been a struggle, I at least have had the chance to learn how to speak effectively to middle-class people. It's been a valuable experience for me, and for them. Most low-income people never have that kind of opportunity.

At PPP we found that written material can be developed in a powerful way without using the language of college-educated people. The foundation grant that we got with the help of Randy Forsberg allowed us to create our educational materials project, flyers and booklets we developed to reach our targeted constituency where the average reading level for adults is third grade. Because we could not find materials about peace issues that we could use with our local folks, we created simple pamphlets that connected issues of concern to our community with military spending. We got our own folks involved in writing the pamphlets. Even those who were illiterate helped by telling us what they thought the pamphlet should say and by making sure the photos communicated the message. Their involvement ensured us that people would understand the materials we were writing. These materials have now been used by groups all over the country.

We have also found that the language used by low-income folks doesn't always have to be translated to communicate clearly to middle-class folks. In San Francisco, for example, PPP's materials have been used to canvass middle-class and wealthy communities. We wrote these brochures for folks who are low-income, but the peace group found our materials to be more effective than the ones they had developed for their college-educated audience. At PPP, we see in this experience an important message for the progressive movement in this country: "Simplify the message." This is not about lowering standards, it is about communication.

The wall of assumptions of knowledge.

The second barrier that low-income people face when attempting to join ranks with middle-class and wealthy people in movements for social change is what I call "assumptions of knowledge." People often wrongly assume that others have the same understanding and information about a problem or issue that they do. These mistaken assumptions are a particularly sensitive issue for low-income people. There are two primary ways that these assumptions are communicated. Sometimes it is done innocently without any intention to hurt or discredit the other person. Other times, people act shocked if you admit that you do not know or understand something.

Within the peace movement, for example, it is often assumed that you should know the names of the peace and justice "leaders" like William Sloane Coffin (former national director of SANE/Freeze). When I first became active in the peace movement, I always left meetings feeling stupid because the group seemed to share information that I did not have. I remember, for example, being shocked when people in the peace group in Charleston made a reference to Japanese-Americans being forced into internment camps within the United States during World War II. When I expressed my lack of knowledge about this, instead of giving me more information, folks responded with disbelief. I felt very badly about myself and wondered why I was so dumb. I now realize that I had never gotten that kind of political education. People in the peace movement assumed that I had the same experiences that they did. For a long time after that incident I didn't dare to question things I did not know about. I just pretended I knew. Now I ask questions and ask for information. I also try to call people on their classism when this kind of thing happens to me.

Another common assumption is that people's life experiences are the same. At a national peace organization board meeting, I stood up and asked that we discuss membership fees that I felt were prohibitive for low-income people. Afterwards, one of the board members, who was a leader in the peace movement, came over to me and tried to explain to me how I wasn't really low-income because, he assumed, I had made a choice to be "downwardly mobile" or low-income by choosing to be an organizer. During those days, most grassroots organizers from the peace movement that I met received little pay as an organizer and many chose to live very simply in order to do the work. It's not that I don't respect middle-class people who choose to live simply. I do. But they need to see that most of them have the option to get out of a hard situation at any time. Most who choose voluntary "poverty" have family resources to fall back on or the education and training that allow them to leave and get a higher paying job if they wish. I discovered that middle-class people commonly assume all organizers share a college education, vacation and travel experience, lots of choices about jobs and schools, and access to health care. Not only did I lack these things, but I felt that the experiences I did have would be seen as less valuable by the people making these assumptions. For low-income folks, who already struggle with feelings of worth because of classism, being faced with a group of people who not only seem to share common knowledge but also wrongly take things for granted is disempowering. People not only often make assumptions about your life experiences, they also assume you share their lifestyle. When I first moved back to rural North Carolina in 1984, I was unable to get public television or public radio in the area where I lived. Only the small local newspaper was available. I learned to depend on news from people who lived in Charlotte or Boston. Middle-class and wealthy people often forget, or have never realized, that access to information, as well as different viewpoints on that information, is a privilege many people in this country do not have.

Many middle-class and wealthy people share the belief that poor people are too busy trying to survive to understand political and economic issues, or to get involved in organizing work even if we do have access to this information. Our experience at PPP has shown us the exact opposite. When political and economic issues are communicated to low-income people in a way that connects to them personally, so that they feel they can really make a difference, they are willing to give lots of time. During the Gulf War in 1990, for example, many of our folks volunteered every evening at the PPP office. After getting off from a long day at the textile mill, they worked to create an educational video, organize a national press conference, and put together educational packets which were mailed all over the country. There is no doubt that they were willing to work so hard because the lives of their own loved ones were at stake. Nearly all of our members had family who were serving in the Gulf War—folks from our community who had joined the military as a way to get an education and a job as a way to a better life.

I have described a few of the assumptions middle-class and wealthy people make about low-income folks. Obviously, these assumptions can work both ways. When I first started speaking to groups in Boston, I often made assumptions about their understanding of low-income people's lives. I assumed they knew more than they did. I was surprised at their shock when I told them about people being refused medical care because they didn't have insurance or their thinking that the Ku Klux Klan was a thing of the past. At first I was offended by these attitudes and felt that people were being deliberately classist. Then I began to realize that the struggles faced by low-income people were actually outside of the reality of most middle-class and wealthy people. In our society, class divisions are so extensive, that middle-class and wealthy people live in a totally different world. Many are unaware of the ways they hurt poor people and have no idea of the impact of their attitudes and choices. I also believe, of course, that there are some people in power who know exactly what they're doing and either don't care or are working to keep class divisions alive in this country.

At the same time, I think it is important to understand that this lack of information about low-income issues did not affect middle-class and wealthy people in the same way as my lack of information affected me. I do not believe that they felt bad about themselves or stupid for not knowing. They did not have problems questioning or even challenging me. They did not feel excluded or less than equal participants. When those in power pass policies which are ignorant of low-income people, they damage our community. My ignorance only affects me but does not have a negative effect on the wealthy.

The wall of simple logistics.

A third barrier to including low-income people in social change movements can be the simple logistics of organizing. This includes how and where meetings are held, how leadership is elected, who makes decisions, how members' participation is maintained, and even how budgets are developed.

The first thing to consider when setting up a meeting or event is the location. It has to be a location that feels comfortable to all who attend and especially to those who traditionally have not been included. It's important to recognize the personal fears of people you are trying to get to a meeting for the first time. If they have never been to the location, it may seem scary or hostile to them. We have had problems, for instance, when we held meetings at the local library. Some people had never been to a library and were afraid of a new and unknown place. Also, because of previous experiences, it was perceived that blacks were not welcome there. In fact, much to our horror, we discovered a mural on the wall of the library meeting room that was very offensive and condescending to blacks. It's important to be aware of how people will perceive the meeting place and to make yourself fully familiar with it as well.

Choosing the right location means allowing people from the constituency you wish to reach to help select the right place. In one instance in North Carolina, a statewide religious organization consulted with us several times about locations for a statewide educational conference they were holding in our area. They had concerns about using a white church, since they were hoping to do outreach into the black community, yet they needed the larger space that only white churches in the area provided. We advised them that our membership could accept their choosing a white church for that reason. However, the church they finally chose was one where a leader of the local Ku Klux Klan held an important position. The group who held the event unknowingly discredited themselves within the black community and didn't understand why they didn't have a large turnout after all the work they had done. Their failure to check out the final decision led to hurt feelings and mistrust on both sides.

Physical accessibility is another major issue in planning meetings for inclusive organizations. It is an especially important issue as you begin to expand your membership to include low-income people for two reasons. First, the conditions that low-income people work and live in create more disability, and second, people who become disabled often become low-income as a result. Doing a good job of making meetings accessible to everyone requires a close knowledge of the group's members and a willingness to understand the particular needs of various disabled people. At PPP, for instance, we know that many members can walk but have a difficult time with stairs. I have seen other groups who were sponsoring events go to great lengths to make them accessible to people with certain disabilities—having a deaf interpreter, for instance, even when there were no deaf people present—while failing to meet the needs of the physically disabled folks who were present.

There are several good rules to follow when choosing a location for a meeting. The meeting space, the bathrooms, and the eating space must all be accessible to disabled people. If you must settle for some part of the meeting space, like the bathroom, not being accessible, let people know. Then disabled folks can make decisions about whether or not to attend the meeting, and about what kind of help they're willing to accept.

Second, be aware that you cannot trust institutions (hotels, restaurants, schools, churches) to be wheelchair accessible even if they say they are. I have been to many events where the organizers were told by the managers of the sites that they were accessible only to learn that there was a step at the front door, or the accessible entrance was locked, or wheelchair accessibility meant going through a busy kitchen and up a freight elevator stacked with serving carts, or the main entrance was accessible but the meeting space was not. It is essential that you check out any site you plan to use and walk through every step that disabled people will use.

I have mentioned problems to consider for wheelchair accessibility, but there are access problems as well for people who are hearing or sight impaired, have environmental and food allergies, or other health considerations. My suggestion is that groups always ask folks what special needs they might have. This might be done by a simple question on a registration form for an event or through a conversation with someone who is attending your meetings. If you cannot meet someone's special need, it is imperative to communicate this inability to the person and to ask their advice on how to best accommodate their needs.

A third critical rule to follow is to carefully consider the logistics of transportation. It is important, if you are meeting in an urban area, to make sure you are near public transportation and that it is safe to travel during the times of the meetings. In rural areas, it is necessary to provide alternative transportation to those you want to reach. At Piedmont Peace Project, providing rides is always part of the organizing turnout plan. Renting buses and vans for important events is a significant item in our budget.

A fourth and extremely important rule to follow when structuring organizations and meetings that are open to people of all classes and races is never forget to provide child care. It is not only essential that child care be available for every meeting, but also necessary that the child care you provide is oriented toward the children. If children are bored or unhappy, it will be harder to get the parents out to future meetings. We at PPP have been told by parents that their *children* made them come because they enjoyed the child care so much. For large and long meetings, like special events and retreats, we often try to include programs for the children so that they are learning some of the same lessons as the adults. For instance, we have used videos, games, and programs that teach about diversity and nonviolence.

A fifth rule that will enable organizations to reach out across class lines involves the schedule of meetings. Many working-class folks, like PPP's members, work very different hours than professional business people. In Kannapolis, a mill town, we hold meetings as early as 5 or 6 P.M. If we held a meeting at 7 or 8 P.M., we would have very little turnout since people have to go to bed early because they get up so early to go to work. Also, we would never have a meeting on Wednesday night since Wednesday is a church night for almost all of our members. When trying to work with different groups it is important to be aware of differences in schedules and to compromise as much as possible. This is an important consideration for committee meetings, as well. I once worked with a group that was serious about bringing low-income folks into their organization and couldn't understand why people wouldn't come to the planning meetings. They held these meetings in the middle of the day since all of them either didn't work or held jobs with flexible hours. They were surprised when I pointed out that most working-class people couldn't come to their planning meetings because they would be at work. It had not occurred to them to ask about people's work schedules, so they couldn't see the barrier that kept people away from their meetings.

The structuring of membership fees is another sensitive area. Most groups are aware of the need to have a sliding scale or a low-income set fee, but experience has shown me that many middle-class organizers need guidance in this area. The sixth rule is to fully understand the impact of your organization's fee structure. For example, some organizations think they are being equitable by giving members a choice between paying a fee or doing volunteer work. In fact this is unequal treatment because only those with money really have a choice. It is also unfair because someone who must choose volunteer work over paying the fee may actually have less time to volunteer than the person who can pay the membership fee.

Middle-class organizers may be trying to reach out to low-income members when they adjust membership fees, but they sometimes do so in ways that are disrespectful. For example, it is important not to separate people into "regular" and "low-income" members. Many organizations provide on their membership forms two different boxes to check off. One box might say "Regular members $25," and the other box, "Low-income members $10." While the difference in fees is a good thing, the categories separate the low-income members *out*.

Why aren't low-income members also "regular members"? This may seem like a small point, but low-income people are sensitive to the subtle ways our social change organizations continue class oppression. A better way is to provide one check box and label it: "Regular membership: $25 ($10 for low-income)." Another possibility is to provide ways for low-income members to pay the membership fee in small amounts, for instance $1 per week.

One of the most common arguments I hear from many groups I work with is that they cannot solve the logistics problems I've described—child care, transportation, disabled access—because they don't have enough money in their budget. I believe that if we are going to be serious about building diverse organizations, we must address these issues. If we are going to work to build diversity, we simply must create the budgets that will allow it to happen. It has to be a priority.

Groups that don't know where to get the money can reach out to individuals and foundations that are particularly interested in funding diversity. An all-volunteer group with a very small budget can do special fund-raisers. For example, our PPP members have held fund-raisers to help pay for transportation and cover other special costs involved in going to events. These fund-raisers allowed folks in the community to be a part of the effort and join in the excitement of the trip. When our group traveled to a national peace conference, we set up a table and sold things our members had made. We let people know that the purchases from our table went to finance our travel expenses. We have held fish-frys to pay for lobbying trips to Washington, D.C., and Gospel Sings to pay for trips to the state capital. Our members are aware of how important these trips are and take responsibility in helping to raise funds to sponsor them.

The wall of meeting format and organizational structure.

A fourth barrier, and one which is often invisible, is the way meetings and organizations are structured. Their structure is critical to people's ability to participate and feel included. One significant problem is that an organization's system for making decisions is often not made clear. How well the decision-making structure is understood can mean the difference between participants feeling empowered and included or shut down and unwanted. Many middle-class people are comfortable with theoretical, impersonal discussion in which people just jump in when they want to speak. This format reflects a college classroom model (and a male model) familiar to those who are college educated. For low-income people (many of whom are women), the approach is unfamiliar, and many do not feel comfortable about entering the discussion. Similarly, in many groups, a lack of explicit structure means that only those people who feel comfortable talking (usually people with privilege) will do so. It's not that low-income people have nothing to say, we just feel that we don't have a way in. Often, people from different cultures and backgrounds need more time to process their thoughts before speaking with "strangers." An inclusive organization will work to find a meeting format that allows everyone to participate. People often assume that because some people process ideas faster they are smarter, but I have learned that people who take more time are usually processing their feelings as well as new information and can have a more complete picture of the situation than those who speak immediately.

The way discussion happens, as well as how decisions are

made, are important considerations in making everyone feel as if they have a voice in the organization. *Robert's Rules of Order*, which are based on the practices and traditions of the British parliament, are followed by many U.S. organizations in their meetings. When I participated in a discussion run according to these rules, I felt that only people who understood the system could fully participate, and that people who were in disagreement with things I wanted to say used the system to stop me from speaking. Even after I learned the Robert's system of rules and how they worked, the system remained a barrier to my full and free participation in discussion. Having a set structure for meetings and maintaining order in discussions are necessary, but there are easier, less alienating ways to achieve these goals. Our practice at PPP and my experience in other organizations have convinced me that using a facilitator is a much simpler, less intimidating, and more supportive way to make sure that all voices are heard.

I have spoken to many groups who use consensus as the way to make decisions. In consensus, a group must come to a shared decision together in which everyone supports the decision. This was the practice, as I've described, in the Quaker meetings I attended as a child, and I found it empowering. However, this approach works only when everyone enters the discussion with an equal voice. It cannot work if some people feel less empowered or less able to articulate their viewpoints. If a person is not comfortable speaking out, then the consensus process is often intimidating. I have participated in many groups where a "consensus" was reached even though some people felt their viewpoint had never been heard and that they had no voice in the final decision. Another problem that can occur when consensus is the only form of decision making for a group is that, if someone comes into the group specifically for the purpose of disrupting its work, that person can effectively block decisions. For groups that are inclusive or want to be inclusive, the democratic process of voting sometimes works better than consensus for making final decisions. It has been my experience that with voting, low-income people tend to feel they have an equal voice in the decision that is made because they have actually participated with their vote. Obviously voting, like consensus, can be disempowering if everyone doesn't have an opportunity to participate in the discussion.

At Piedmont Peace Project, we combine voting with consensus building. We make sure everyone has a chance to participate in the discussion and we give time to people who have not spoken. We work for agreement before a vote is actually taken, and we would never move forward on a decision that won with only one or two votes without further discussion. In this way, we are following many of the principles of consensus building but are using the vote process to help ensure we have a true consensus.

Communication across lines of race, class, gender, and sexual orientation is not easy to build. In structuring meetings, it is essential to give each person all the time she or he needs to speak. For many people who have not had the experience of talking in a group or are talking to people from different class, race, and gender backgrounds, the process can be painful and slow. It is very important not to jump in and finish sentences for people or to interrupt them. Interruptions can easily take away a person's voice. In PPP, we train organizers to count to seventeen after they have asked a general question or while they are waiting for a response from someone. They must count to seventeen before saying anything. Usually, someone responds before the organizer gets to seventeen.

It is important when reaching out to low-income folks, or anyone else for that matter, that meetings be about *accomplishing* something. It is important to give people an "action" assignment in every meeting. Low-income people especially need to see concretely that they are making a difference before they will believe it. Many groups give educational programs without any actions assigned, believing that knowledge about a particular issue is enough to make people work for change. But I believe that if folks leave a program without understanding what to do with the knowledge they have gained, they frequently feel even more disempowered.

People in our communities do not respond to a regular monthly meeting unless they know that there is a reason for it and that something is going to get done. People are much more willing to come to a called meeting for a particular purpose. In fact, if there is an urgent matter to be dealt with people are willing to come much more often than on a monthly basis. When we have been in the middle of a campaign, we have had weekly (and at times every other day) meetings with excellent attendance. In one of our counties, we hold a regular monthly meeting just for the steering committee, but all other meetings are based on current action needs.

The way a group elects leadership is crucial in broadening its membership to new people. There are several issues to consider. The first is being clear and informative about what the jobs and responsibilities are for officers or leaders to be elected. Such responsibility may be scary or alienating to a potentially effective new leader; our organizations need to be more flexible and open to new ways of thinking about leadership positions. Can it be a shared position? Can two positions be created from one, allowing more people to use their skills to participate? The second issue is recruitment. Many people, especially low-income people, people of color, and women, have been taught that they are not leaders. Current leaders and organizers must see it as their job to help support new leadership until new people feel comfortable on their own. Groups should offer training and support to promote new and different leadership. It is important to set affirmative action goals with a time table for meeting those goals. As I've said before, the board of directors at PPP is required to be at least two-thirds people of color, two-thirds women, and two-thirds low-income people. This proportion is representative of our membership and also allows those who are traditionally most oppressed to assume leadership roles.

In conclusion I want to say that even at Piedmont Peace Project, where we have had years of practice in bridging class, color, gender, and other dividing lines, we still must constantly remind ourselves to look carefully for the "invisible walls" that separate us. It is much easier to propose ways to bring down these walls than it is to put your shoulder to the task. But we're committed to figuring out ways to do better work, to teaching others, and to holding each other accountable to working in these better ways. We caution others not to expect to be able to make all of these changes at once, and not to think these walls fall down easily. They don't.

In talking about the "invisible walls" created by class prejudice, and other forms of oppression, my aim has been to help all of us realize that they do exist. We must begin to look for these walls, and when we find them, explore ways to remove them. Only when we begin to replace these walls with well-built bridges will we begin to approach our goal of building a diverse movement. It won't happen immediately. We have years of mistrust and misunderstanding to overcome. We need to begin to learn more about each other and respect the differences we have among us. The respect and acceptance we learn will open the door for the different gifts we each bring to this work and will allow us to develop new leadership to carry us forward. In the next chapter, I explore what a new leadership that is inclusive looks like and how we can begin to develop that leadership.

8

....

Redefining Leadership

WHEN I FIRST STARTED to talk about peace issues and the concerns of my community, I was advised by middle-class people that I wasn't the right spokesperson. But I found that my words and my life experiences connected to other people's experience. I knew I didn't fit the "traditional" definition of a leader—the white educated male who talked facts and statistics, not feelings and experiences. I was a low-income woman who used the words of my community to share my feelings and experiences. When I spoke truthfully and honestly about what I saw and how things needed to change, people in my community wanted to join in. I began to realize that people in my community were looking to me as a leader. Because of my own experiences, I realized that there could be, and in fact, had to be, a different definition of a leader. As a result, when I founded PPP, one of the most important things I promised was that we would work to make everyone feel that she or he could be a leader. Instead of using the traditional structure of leadership, with one person at the top, we set out to define a new vision of leaders and leadership.

Redefining leadership is really a survival issue for people of color, women, and low-income communities. Traditional leadership has historically excluded us for the most part. Most of the exceptions are people who have been recognized because the traditional leaders in the power structure have identified them as representatives of our communities. Often these people have ended up being co-opted (they have taken on the identity and values of those in power); sometimes they have been chosen to begin with because they looked or acted more like people in the power structure than people in low-income communities. You can see that this is the opposite of low-income people finding our voices. To preserve our communities and the integrity of our lives, we must find leaders outside the traditional power structure.

Even within progressive organizations we need to redefine leadership. The most common leadership model does not encourage people to become leaders. Organizations usually have a single leader, and even if that person is very positive and in touch with the community, everyone else becomes dependent on that one individual. If something happens to that person the organization will likely fall apart. At PPP, we have worked toward building a model of shared leadership.

Out of an organization that develops many leaders come many strategies, styles, and ideas for making change. This variety makes an organization more vital and more likely to reach lots of different people. In contrast, if one leader defines an organization, then only the people who can identify with that single person will feel included. If one leader makes the decisions on how things should be done, the strategies become limited to a single personal style. In the early years of PPP, I used to think that I needed to let other people do things their way so that they would learn from their own mistakes. What I learned, though, is that there are a lot of *different* ways to successfully reach a goal. I would think I knew the "best way," only to find out that a totally different approach was even more successful. Through the shared leadership model at PPP, I've learned from others new ways to do our work. And I have also learned how important it is to have a range of different approaches to draw upon in achieving our goals.

The most powerful leadership occurs when other members identify with the leader and feel that they could also work in that role. Leaders are more effective when other people can say, "Oh, I can do that" or "That's just how I feel too" —instead of focusing on what a brilliant or exceptional person the leader is. Traditionally leaders are seen as separate from their communities. They're regarded as smarter, more talented, more powerful people whose individual personalities set them apart. But if a leader truly shares an identity with other people, then the people see they have something in common with a leader and together, they move forward.

It is often said that there are too many leaders and not enough followers. It is also said that leaders are born, not made. Both of these sayings come out of a traditional model of leadership that honors hierarchical power and class status. In economic systems like capitalism, where only a few people can be at the top (those who own the companies) and most people have to be at the bottom, a system with few leaders "works." You don't want too many leaders or shared leadership because the structure requires lots of followers. People have come to think that this system is "normal" or natural because it is so promoted and accepted in the United States.

If progressive groups are to begin to help bridge the divisions that currently exist in the United States, our view of leadership must reflect a different vision of society—one rooted in real economic and social democracy. This new view of what constitutes a leader and leadership will require us to honor several principles. First, the idea that, while leaders have traditionally been white, male and middle-class people, we are committed to building an organization of diverse leaders and to making it possible for anyone to become a leader. Second, that *all* people *can* learn to be leaders through support and training in which people get to recognize themselves as leaders and learn the skills of leadership. And third, that shared leadership is the result of shared decision making. We must believe in many leaders.

In order to put into practice these principles, PPP has built a model based on sharing power and created a structure for broad-based leadership. Through our organizing work, our staffing, and our workshops, we have consciously challenged the ways that traditional ideas about leadership have kept our members, and people like us, from recognizing their own power and their own potential to be leaders.

At PPP, our training workshops help our members look at who the traditional leaders in this country are. We ask people to name those who are in power and list the skills that they feel those people have as leaders. The list usually includes things like being able to speak in public, writing skills, and being able to deal with media. Then we look within our own group to see which of these skills we have *as a group*. We may not have one person who possesses all these different skills, but almost always together we possess all of the different skills that people have listed. Then we ask *why* the people in power have power. Often, we discover that the reason isn't just the skills we've listed but some additional reason: the person has money or is white or has a certain educational level or is male. You might think this process would discourage members, but it actually helps them analyze what parts of our idea of leadership are based on skills and what parts are based on privilege. It is the first step to beginning to think of *ourselves* as leaders.

The next step we take is to redefine how a person becomes a leader. At PPP we believe that leadership can be taught. For instance, since dealing with the media is an important leadership skill in our organization, we find the person within our group who can begin to teach that skill to everyone else. This is a very different perspective from the traditional one that sees leaders as "born, not made." We are committed to following a pattern that allows many new leaders to be "made."

When traditional leaders make speeches, to take another example, they tend to use all sorts of facts and quote statistics. When we teach public speaking at PPP, we emphasize speaking from the heart, speaking from experience and telling our own stories. We also work to recognize that we do not have to speak in a particular way. In fact, trying to talk like people think a leader should talk, like using "standard" grammar, can actually stop us from being articulate and from speaking with our own power.

In teaching public speaking, we work in teams and allow people to choose their teammates. Usually, teams consist of people whose skills or talents differ. Someone with a lot of enthusiasm and good ideas but who doesn't write well may work with another person who can write. Someone who is afraid or shy will team up with someone who is more outgoing. The pairs work up a joint presentation: the more outgoing person might speak first, but the other person will present also. In this way, both people have input into creating the final presentation. We also talk about how to deal with our feelings, especially nervousness. We tell people not to try to pretend it is not there, but to acknowledge it—to say "This is the first time I have ever spoken in front of a group like this and I am very nervous about it" as a way to be more comfortable.

If we are presenting to an "outside" audience, the final step in our training workshop is to get our folks to "translate" their speeches. We ask our members to think what needs to be translated for middle-class folks to understand us. The outcome is still powerful because it comes from the heart, and the process of translating is done in an empowering way. Even though the final words may not be the way we speak at home, folks totally understand why we're changing them and that they are the "expert" translators themselves.

In addition to building leadership through workshops, we promote new leadership within our organizing work. New leadership sometimes emerges in very unexpected places. For example, a very quiet, shy, older woman, whom I'll call "Doris," came to PPP's first open house. She wanted to volunteer. We had a list of tasks from stuffing envelopes to making phone calls to helping lobby to going to events, but Doris would only volunteer to clean the office and do yard work. We let her clean, but we also talked about her as a staff. When we see a volunteer who will only do domestic tasks, our goal is to give that person an opportunity to move beyond that role. Doris had a lot of potential, but she was nervous and afraid. We decided to ask her to come to a "Get Out the Vote" workshop. We asked our trainer to pay special attention to Doris and to try to get her involved without making her feel overwhelmed. During the workshop, our trainer finally got Doris to agree to do a role play in which she asked other people to volunteer to work. He stayed with her and supported her, and she did it. Afterwards, Doris was incredibly excited and so happy and proud of herself. The following fall, one of our leaders ended up in the hospital on "Get Out the Vote" day, and Doris took on the job. She organized her whole community by going door to door, recruiting volunteers, and setting up rides to get out the vote. Doris had found her voice. Her story is just one example of the ways I have seen leadership develop in people when they are given the chance to break out of old roles. It's important to recognize that Doris not only became a leader at PPP—the experience changed her life in many ways.

Another way that we try to break the traditional leadership mold in our organizing is by having the people who have become leaders become the trainers for the new leaders. We also ask volunteers to begin to teach others organizing skills they have learned. For example, once I was speaking with a woman who had consistently turned out ten volunteers. I said, "OK, you've been getting out ten people for 'Get Out the Vote' day. Now it's time to get out a hundred." She said, "Forget that." And we just made a joke about it. Then I said, "No, in all seriousness, here is what I think we could do. What if you were able to get your ten folks to each do what you are doing? Then you don't make any more phone calls than before. Instead of getting them to get out the vote, your job is to get each of them to get ten other people to do what they've been doing." We discussed how she might ask them to volunteer and what kind of training they might need. She agreed to try to get her ten volunteers to come to a training workshop, and she was very excited to think her ten calls might eventually bring in one hundred people.

The rewards of traditional leadership are rewards to the individual ego—getting strokes for "my" idea, "my program," "my total dollars raised." At PPP, we see it differently—the reward of leadership lies in giving what you've learned to others. People are recognized as leaders at PPP not for any single event they've organized, but for the new people they have motivated to join the organization through their leadership example.

Recognizing new leaders is an important process. The first principle is to not make any assumptions about who will or will not be a leader. Recognizing new leadership means being very observant and being ready to react when a person seems ready to take a next step toward becoming a leader. When people say no, it is often not because they don't want to be involved. They are often afraid, or have other issues that keep them from believing they can make a difference. My assumption is always that people want to take on leadership responsibilities and want to move forward to make things happen. That is what I mean when I say we must look at everyone as a potential leader.

A good example of this willingness to believe that people want to be leaders is the way in which our organizer George Friday handled our first organizing meeting in Asheville, North Carolina. Only three of the expected sixteen people showed up for that workshop. Each of the three was somewhat quiet and made references to past failed attempts to organize their community. George could have spent the time waiting and disrespected the three who came by focusing on those who hadn't showed up. Instead, she took the time to appreciate each person and their commitment to being there. She spent several hours going through the original agenda including discussing who leaders could be and encouraging folks to share their visions for their community. She then brought up planning the next meeting and developing a list of who should be invited. All three of the folks were now enthusiastic and saw themselves as important and felt confident that they could bring others. When the next meeting happened, twenty-five people came and the three original folks were there as "leaders."

Just as important as recognizing new leadership is encouraging new leaders along the way by acknowledging and valuing their accomplishments. Most low-income folks and many women have a difficult time understanding that their actions have real results. Even when they see the results, it is hard for them to accept that they were responsible. It is important to help people see their own impact in order for them to begin to develop as leaders. For example, after "Doris" organized the get-out-the-vote efforts in her community, we told her, "You made this happen. If you had not got volunteers to go to every door and ask people to vote, probably only half of that number would have voted. And, if you had not got volunteers to drive people to the polls, many who really wanted to vote would not have had the opportunity. *You* made this happen." Telling people explicitly what they did and the result of their efforts allows them to believe they can make a difference. Sometimes, just asking the question "What do you think would have happened had you not done that?" helps people see what they were able to accomplish. Calling their attention to their contribution is extremely important to creating leadership. In our society we often assume that if someone does a job well, they're just doing their job—there is no need to let them know that they are doing valuable work. We are only too willing to criticize—but not to praise or respect people's efforts. At PPP we always try to acknowledge people's efforts. We all need that.

The definition of leadership we put into practice at PPP is not without some problems. Sometimes the most difficult work we do is supporting people along their way to becoming leaders. It is tempting to give a task to a volunteer and just say "do it," but to build leadership, we all need to share in the task by giving each other ongoing support. Support may mean giving encouragement and appreciation even when a task gets only half done. It may mean pitching in and sharing the task if another person seems overwhelmed or too scared to continue. Frequently we must call and check in with volunteers who have agreed to take on a particular task. If it is not happening, we don't assume that the person is too busy or just doesn't care. We assume that there is a way we need to support them. They really want to do it; otherwise they wouldn't have volunteered. A lot of people want to make those ten phone calls but then they get scared. Sometimes it just means a phone call to talk them through their feelings. This kind of encouragement takes time and attention away from other tasks that seem more important, and all of us at PPP have failed to check in with volunteers and then gotten upset when the work didn't get done. We have to constantly remind ourselves that every member and every volunteer is a potential leader.

As I've said before, one of the issues we have struggled with in building a new style of leadership at PPP is sexism. The tendency to think of leaders only as white middle-class men is as true within progressive organizations as it is in other areas of society. It remains true even though there are more women working in progressive organizations and in the overall workforce now than in the past. I'd like to describe the kind of leadership in fighting sexism that was shown by women at a conference on voter registration that PPP staff and members attended. The male participants at this conference wouldn't let the women in attendance speak. They interrupted us and spoke out of turn, but the male facilitator would let the men talk as long as they liked. I saw all the women around me just shut down. Some of us talked about it and decided that we should do something. We passed a note around to all the women during the middle of the session to tell them to meet in a side room before we went to lunch.

When we broke for lunch, all of the women gathered in the room. We talked about what we were feeling. Several women were very articulate and objected to specific actions as sexist. Others admitted feeling confused or angry but hadn't seen the behavior of the men as sexism. We decided on an action to take: any time someone said something sexist or acted sexist, we would all stand up. A white middle-class woman asked, "How will we know if it is sexist? And what if I think it is sexist and you don't?" I remembered attending other gatherings where the women's caucuses were very divided and worried that we'd fail to act because we couldn't agree, when a PPP member said, "Well, we all have to stick together on this. If any one person thinks it's sexist, whether I see it or not, we all stand up together. It doesn't matter, if one woman stands up, we all stand up." And that was what we did. When we all stood up, one person explained what we were doing. Some of the men got very angry, and others acknowledged and supported us by standing with us.

As a result of our leadership, one of the men who was to lead a workshop challenged us to use his time for whatever we wanted to do. We seized the opportunity to do a workshop on sexism. We did an exercise in which the men listened to how the women felt when they were treated as we had been in the conference. Then we gave them a chance to respond. Several men were angry, and a couple even left the workshop early. But many men said they learned from the experience. One even said it changed his life and would change the way he worked with women in the future.

We take on the issue of sexism in our own PPP workshops when helping our members learn new leadership models. Our experience in the communities PPP works in has taught us that, while women in these communities may actually do most of the volunteer work for a specific PPP campaign or project, these same women often do not see themselves as leaders. Again and again, they will choose men as their spokespersons or as members of the PPP steering committee for their community. Sometimes they will choose men who do none of the door-to-door, or telephone, or other community work and who participate only in the sense of expressing their views at meetings. Their views are often treated by the women present as authoritative, simply because men have expressed them.

At PPP, we began to see this pattern as a problem and to think how we might help our women members identify themselves as leaders. For example, when one community group needed to choose a steering committee, we asked all the members to choose the five *people* who did the most work for the group. After five women were named and stood up in the meeting, we asked the members whether any of these women should be on the steering committee. After the women agreed to serve on the steering committee and were approved by the members, we asked the members to choose the five *men* they thought did the most work for the group. These men were also approved as steering committee members. This approach allowed the PPP members to begin to see a different leadership model—one that tied leadership to work rather than gender. It was a revolutionary idea for folks, and exhilarated them in the way it released them from choosing leaders whom they sometimes did not respect nor feel were true representatives. It permitted them to empower themselves to become leaders.

Confronting the kinds of oppression—like sexism—that exist within progressive groups and organizations is difficult but also critically important. By being made aware of how they may be giving up their power, women and others may find new ways to understand the behaviors of people in their own organization and outside it. A new or renewed understanding of how sexism, homophobia, racism, and other forms of oppression are at work all around us is a necessary part of PPP's redefinition of leadership. Leaders allow all voices to be heard.

When I talk to people who are struggling to develop their own leadership, I tell about my own struggle to believe I could be a leader. People see me now as a leader, though I keep reminding them that I am no different than other people in our community. I do not pretend that I have always had the skills that I have now. This is important to communicate to people who are beginning to develop their own leadership skills. I once found in tears two of our PPP staff who were writing their speeches to deliver at a fund-raising event. They felt afraid that they could not do their speeches exactly the same way I give a speech now: without notes and without seeming to have any fear or nervousness about it. So what I said to them was, "I didn't start out this way. What I had to do when I first started was to write out word for word what I was going to say. I memorized it and then I took my cards with me. I mostly read my speeches in the beginning." I talked about how I felt then and how I would cry every time I had to do a speech. They had seen me speak after five years of regular speech-making and felt that they had to do the same. This was very disempowering and only through sharing my story were they able to feel they could then develop their own way of speaking. To model leadership, those of us who are seen as leaders must always remember how we got to where we are now, and we must constantly turn to others to teach them the first step.

Because of my traveling around and now writing this book, a lot of people want to see me as the "only" leader for PPP. They think that I must be the exception. I know this isn't true because of working with an entire staff of leaders. I know this isn't true because of all the leaders who are in every community PPP serves. "Shared leadership" is a real and essential part of the structure of PPP and continually renews our belief that all of us are leaders in our own way.

People often ask us at PPP if we have a problem with too many leaders. We have a series of joint management teams for the office, training, and staff; advisory committees for each community which share decision-making powers with community people; a committee for each event which includes staff, community leaders, and new people coming into the leadership; and finally, the overall structure of PPP is governed by a combination of community folks, supporters, and staff.

I suppose from a traditional perspective on power and leadership, that might look like too many leaders. But our experience at PPP has shown us that the more leaders we have, the more we share leadership, and the more new people we have taking on leadership roles, the stronger and more powerful we become. I think of leadership as being an expanding circle. The more the circle enlarges to include, the bigger and more powerful it grows, and the stronger the organization becomes.

9

Getting Smart about Organizing

MANY GROUPS INVOLVED IN organizing for social change have chosen not to use techniques and skills identified as coming from the corporate world or as being typical of government policies because such methods appear to undermine the basic principles of these groups. This is a very real and understandable fear, and at PPP, we have had similar concerns. However, we have learned that we can adapt to our needs some of what businesses do without compromising our values.

In this chapter I want to look at some of the prejudices against standard business practices that exist in the progressive movement and how they keep us from accomplishing real change.

The media.

One of the progressive movement's strongest prejudices has always concerned the media. Like many progressive groups,

PPP was wary about the media when we first began organizing. Newspaper, television, and radio always seemed to do negative stories about PPP, if and when they bothered to do anything at all. Based on similar experiences, some progressive groups have simply abandoned the media. That's how we felt in the beginning too. But then we realized that we were actually shooting ourselves in the foot, and we began to try to think smart about the media—about how we could make it work for us.

Prior to 1989, a few news stories were written about PPP. They were largely accurate, but not particularly helpful and not written from our perspective. Then, in 1989, PPP won the Peace Development Fund's national Grassroots Peace Award. Part of the award was the part-time service for three months of a media consultant. The consultant proposed coming to North Carolina to arrange a press conference about our winning the award. I was convinced that a press conference would never work to our advantage. The local media, I told the consultant, was terrible. They never covered us. But she persuaded me that we could get good coverage. She came to us for two weeks, and during that time I learned an enormous amount about the media and even about how the most conservative newspapers in our local communities could be convinced to run positive stories on PPP. This experience so changed the way I thought about the media that I talked to the consultant about doing ongoing work for PPP. Soon PPP, which had been close to shutting the door forever on the press, had hired a media consultant and developed a three-part media strategy.

The first way we use the media is to support our organizing goals. First we determine our targets for a media campaign, and then we figure out how to use the media to focus on those targets in ways that will benefit our organizing efforts.

Here is an example from the Proctor-Silex campaign. PPP placed an article about the closing of the Moore County Proctor-Silex plant in the local newspaper of a teeny little town up in Ohio. Why? Because the chair of the board of the Proctor-Silex Corporation lived in that community, and we wanted to get a message out to his neighbors about what he was doing in North Carolina, so that he would feel pressured to listen to us. We arranged for similar media coverage of other Proctor-Silex board members—one was the chair of the board of the Nature Conservancy, a national environmental organization, and another was on the board of another national environmental organization. Since Proctor-Silex was leaving a large toxic waste dump behind when they closed in our community, we targeted them in the environmental media in order to pressure them into paying attention to our demands.

We always work to get fully developed stories, written by journalists, which reflect our point of view. To get these stories, we try to develop credibility and professional relationships with reporters and to meet "their" criteria of what makes a good story. Oftentimes things happen at PPP that we think are newsworthy—our membership conference, for instance—but this event would not meet the criteria of "news worthiness" for a reporter. We have learned that it is important to understand what kind of story is considered newsworthy in order to build credibility with a media source. Once credibility is established there is a better chance the reporter will continue to cover important events and trust us for leads on stories.

We also work to make sure our stories are strategically

placed for the most impact. For instance, during the Proctor-Silex campaign the story about the board member who was also on the board of the Nature Conservancy went twice into the progressive weekly newspaper, *In These Times*, but it also got into the *Los Angeles Times* and then was picked up by the Associated Press. All of these stories were told from our point of view. If we had written our own story, it would not have had the same credibility, and I doubt the *Los Angeles Times* or other papers would have run it. Having a media consultant who knew how to market our story made the difference.

In using the media to support our organizing goals, we've also discovered how good coverage by the press helps empower people and develop their leadership abilities. Seeing your own words in the newspaper can be incredibly powerful and has helped our members feel that they could really make their voices heard. There is also a great feeling of power that comes from seeing other low-income people's words in print. It is empowering to know that people like us are being reflected in the media.

The second way that we use the media is to support our fund-raising. Any local organizing coverage we get is shown to donors and foundations so that they understand that our work is making progress. You can't get media coverage if things aren't really happening. You have to be doing the work. We also aim to place stories in places that we think will support our fund-raising. For example, a story in the *Unitarian Universalist World* magazine does not help PPP's local organizing. None of our folks read that magazine, and we don't have many Unitarian Universalists in our area. But many of PPP's donors are Unitarian Universalists, and they will see that article. It is important to communicate directly to donors about what you are doing and involve them in your work. We look carefully at media that our donors read and listen to and include those publications in our media outreach.

The third, and I think probably the most important work we do with the media, is not about getting any kind of recognition for PPP. It is about changing the way the media usually reports on issues we are concerned about. We want to redefine the way the media sees low-income people. Often the media reports on issues of concern to low-income people in a very unbalanced way. For instance, stories about the North American Free Trade Agreement (NAFTA) and about the impact of plant closings are almost always reported from the point of view of corporations. We sat down and tried to think about how we could begin to change the perspectives of both our local and state media. (We didn't think we could change national media, at that point.) We decided that we wanted to become a source; we wanted to be among the experts the media called on when they had questions about particular issues.

Becoming an expert that the media trusted meant we had to be willing to support stories that had nothing to do with PPP. For example, if a reporter we knew brought up an issue for a story, we would volunteer to help the reporter find people to talk about the issue, without ever saying, "And we want our name in it." During the Proctor-Silex campaign, we worked to establish ourselves as expert on the impact of NAFTA without turning the media's attention to PPP. We began by providing documented information to the media. We brought to North Carolina an expert from a Chicago research center that dealt with the economic impact of plant closings on communities. We held a press conference with staff and members to report the expert's opinion on how the Proctor-

Silex plant closing was going to affect our community. The expert was quoted in the press, but not in connection with PPP. Some of the stories included a line or two about PPP, but we did not aim for that exposure. Our primary purpose was to be seen as a credible source. One outcome was that several local elected officials who had not supported our work before began to work with us after the Chicago expert's findings were reported in the paper.

Our strategy of keeping the spotlight on NAFTA worked. On 14 November 1993, just before the vote on NAFTA, the *Raleigh News & Observer* ran a three-page story called "The Faces of NAFTA." One of the people quoted in that story was a PPP member. The story never mentioned PPP, but it was told from our point of view. We called the reporter to tell him that we really appreciated being asked to help with the story and asked why he had thought to call us. "I had no choice," he said. "We have these data banks on past news stories organized by topic. I plugged in labor and NAFTA, and PPP's name showed up sixteen times." If we had chosen to work with reporters only when they were going to write about PPP, it would have hurt the amount of coverage we get for our organization. At year's end our local newspapers publish recaps of the year's big news stories. PPP's name appears only two or three, or perhaps as many as five times in these recaps. But we can usually point to one-third of the stories as stories that PPP has influenced in one way or another.

Strategic planning.

Another bias of some progressive organizations is against the kind of strategic planning that characterizes successful business operations. But at PPP we are thinking smart about many of these planning techniques. Planning—from setting organization goals all the way down to setting weekly work schedules for our staff—allows us to know both when we have had a victory and when we need to be setting new goals. At PPP, we start by forming a shared vision of what our work is to be in the future. Then we create five-year plans to achieve that vision. These five-year plans are broken down into one-year plans, which we translate into plans for months, weeks, and days. Out of this general organizational work plan, each staff member creates an individual work plan. These individual plans are used in several ways. At the beginning of each month, staff members present their monthly work plans to the management team. Each plan is reviewed by the staff supervisor, who offers suggestions for structuring realistic plans with achievable goals. At PPP, a staff member's failure to follow these work plans without notification is grounds for termination. The work plans help create accountability among the staff. Otherwise, we've found, as many organizations do, that it is easy to get distracted by the needs and demands of others. Then, nobody's agenda gets carried out.

The second use for the work plan is to make sure that people get enough vacation time. A common problem, especially among progressive organizers and activists, is that people will work themselves into the ground. Partly, we create these plans so that staff members will plan vacation time and have enough personal time to reflect on their own lives. Without a work plan it's more likely that people will "burn out." In some cases, PPP work plans ensure that folks spend enough time working for the organization. Ensuring that folks take enough time off so that they will continue to be long-term productive employees is a departure from the way that most companies or organizations use work plans, but it is a key use if we plan to build a movement for lasting change. We also use "work" plans to help people map out not just vacation periods, but also ways of taking care of themselves. This includes fun time, relaxation, therapy, massage—all are examples of ways of honoring the self. If people can't think of ways to honor themselves, the staff supervisor makes suggestions to point them toward these goals too!

PPP's work plans grew out of my own experience as a supervisor. In the beginning I found it difficult to hold people accountable in an ongoing way. I had a tendency to let things slide until they got really bad, an experience I now know is not unusual. The practice of creating individual work plans has been extremely helpful in holding us all accountable, has helped us set realistic organizational goals, and helped us all work at our own best pace.

With a strategic plan, an organization can be more flexible and, as a result, more effective. For instance, the Gulf War was an "unplanned" event for PPP, as it was for everyone. But with an overall strategic plan in place, we were able to shape our "emergency" work regarding the Gulf War in ways that still worked to meet our overall long-term goals. Also, having an overall plan enabled us to make informed choices about what work we would put off in order to deal with the Gulf War. We were able to see the consequences and make our choices accordingly.

I often tell organizers that having a long-term strategic plan is like having a budget. Having a good budget doesn't mean you never blow your budget, but when you do blow it, you know what you need to do about it, like pay the power bill two weeks late. A strategic plan helps prevent you from going into a crisis mode, where you quickly become frantic and eventually burn out.

Many social change organizations are desperate for strategic planning. There is not the same resistance to strategic planning as there is to a media strategy, but people working for social change often want to make everything happen at once and resist sitting down to set reasonable goals and objectives. Our experience at PPP is that only by developing a detailed strategic plan can an organization realistically expect to make anything happen.

Needs of the staff.

A third way that we try to think smart about organizing is in addressing the needs of our staff. Our work on internalized oppression is one way we do this. We are also concerned about keeping a good balance between the demands of our workloads and our personal lives. We try to think abut doing our work in a way that allows time for family and personal pursuits.

How we pay our staff is a critical issue. In many social change organizations, there is a tendency to pay very low salaries without benefits. Low salaries often mean that good people cannot afford to work for organizations or that they will move on quickly because they must find careers that pay enough to meet their personal and family needs. Low salaries also prevent organizations from building diverse staffs. One national community organization, for instance, actually had a policy of paying below minimum wage to their organizers. Therefore the people who became organizers with this group were mostly young and middle-class with family who would support them in case of illness. The low wages restricted low-income people from being able to do organizing, especially low-income people who had families.

We want the people we are organizing to have fair wages—we should have the same standard for ourselves. We do valuable work and we deserve decent pay. Most labor unions, for example, have recognized that organizers should be paid decent wages. I have consulted with a group where the organizers are paid very low wages, below minimum wage. I raised this as an issue and was told by the leadership (who are not paid) that they didn't feel it was fair to pay the organizers more than the members of the organization make. This organization works for better conditions and better pay for its members, but at the same time, as a matter of principle, they force their organizers to work under the same unjust conditions. I believe all social change organizations should become models for what we are trying to create in our communities.

Benefits are also a part of keeping people in organizing for the long term and of allowing people who don't have access to health care benefits to join the organization. At PPP, because we believe our work is for the long term, we have life insurance and pension plans. Though we have not been able to afford a full-fledged pension plan yet, we have started a plan at the minimum percentage of coverage. It's a start. Our hope is to raise the coverage to what a regular pension would be in a corporation. The point is that we have made decent salaries and benefits part of our organization's goals, something we are working toward. Creating a good working situation for individuals will benefit the movement that we are building in the long run.

Fund-raising, budgets, and marketing.

Where to get the money for improved salaries and benefits leads us to fund-raising, budgets, and marketing, another area where progressive organizations need to get smart and overcome their biases against simple business practices. I have asked many organizations what their budgets are; they answer that their budget is basically whatever they can raise. Then I ask how they know how much to raise. "We raise whatever we can," they say, "and that is our budget." At PPP we spend a lot of time figuring out how much it will cost to accomplish our strategic plan. Every year our budget gets more detailed and more accurate. A budget that reflects the organization's strategic plan allows a group to raise funds more effectively. We approach potential donors with specific needs; for instance, we tell them we need $10,000 because we are going to rent forty-two vans at a total cost of $4,200, provide food for more than two hundred volunteers, purchase gas for one hundred volunteer cars, pay printing costs for pamphlets—all of which will get seventy-five hundred people to the polls on election day. This kind of detailed list lets donors see why they should give us $10,000. They know exactly how their money is being spent. Without a strategic plan and a budget that reflects that plan, you cannot raise the kind of money that is needed. It is always a struggle to raise money, there is no doubt about that. But one of the reasons PPP has been effective in raising the money we need every year has been that we have had a strategic plan *and* a budget.

A strategic plan and a budget are particularly critical during difficult economic times. For example, 1991 and 1992 were especially challenging years for groups in the South. PPP also suffered and was forced to lay off a staff person. We did everything in our power as staff to arrange emergency fund-raising to make sure PPP's program kept moving forward. But it was only because we had a strategic plan and a budget in place that we were able to make efficient use of our resources and not go into the red.

In addition to a fund-raising plan, it is important for organizations to have a marketing plan. Marketing is usually thought of in terms of selling products. But I think of marketing as figuring out how to talk about your work and get the message of what you are doing across to particular groups of people. When you are organizing, you are literally marketing a message.

Fund-raising involves looking first at what we believe and how we want to raise money, but we must also think about who our audiences are and how we can make them understand our message. As low-income people, we need to think particularly about how to translate our message into terms that middle-class and upper-class donors can understand. We're not changing the message, we're *marketing* the message. For example, PPP has a five-year marketing plan. We realized that we needed to double our budget in five years in order to meet our goals, so we looked first at how to develop new markets. We began to think about who our potential new donors might be and to develop a plan to reach these people, educate them about our issues, and begin to turn them into donors. Second, we looked at how to increase the amount of money we get from our current donors. "Why are they giving us money in the first place?" we asked. What do *they* see as their long-term vision? Thinking about our donors' points of view enabled us to talk about our work in ways they could under-stand. Marketing our message has led us to bring donors on visits to our area, in order to give them a broader understand-ing of our work. And we have also done diversity workshops on classism and racism with our donors so that they recognize these issues and learn constructive responses to them. These workshops were risky because they challenge the participants' own attitudes, but although we have lost a few donors this way, we have gained much more in the long term. These workshops have built a stronger and more supportive rela-tionship with our donors.

Communicating with foundations.

Finally, in getting smart about organizing, we have had to think about our relationship to foundations. I think the big-gest challenge social change organizations face, especially low-income organizations, is how to communicate with founda-tions that offer funding. The requirements many foundations have for writing proposals and reports are often extremely difficult for low-income folks (and maybe for other folks as well) to meet. The language that foundations use can be very alienating. At PPP, we have worked hard to develop relation-ships with people who work at foundations whom we can talk to about problems created by their use of technical language, and whom we can educate about PPP's economic and social justice concerns.

Organizations in search of funding often try to figure out what foundations want to hear, rather than being honest about their concerns and needs. They struggle to meet the conditions necessary to get the funding without being dishonest about their own priorities. Certainly we have struggled with this difficult balance at PPP. But I think it would be wiser to challenge foundations to change the way they relate to social change organizations, and particularly to low-income groups.

Part of being honest with foundations is being realistic about how much the work costs. At PPP, we present foundations with a plan and a realistic budget. We're found that, for the most part, they respect us for being honest about what we think we can achieve on a specific budget. I've worked and consulted with organizations whose staff and board felt that they were obligated to carry out a program even if they received only half the money that they requested. This leads to unrealistic expectations on the part of the foundations and to staff burnout. At PPP we tell foundations that they cannot expect us to provide the same program with half the funding. We explain that, if they can give us only half the money we need, and we are unable to raise the money elsewhere, we will be able to conduct the training program in only three counties and not in the six counties originally proposed.

Being honest with foundations often amounts to educating them. For example, one national voter registration group set the cost of registering one person to vote at $2, and that figure became a standard among foundations that fund this kind of work. When PPP started doing voter registration work, we quickly realized it was not possible to get this work done in a low-income rural area for only $2 per registered voter. In fact, the cost for us was averaging about $5 a person. This cost included, among other things, transportation, three door-to-door contacts, printed materials, and volunteer expenses. We tried to show these costs to foundations, but they were very reluctant to abandon the $2 standard. So we were faced with the challenge of competing against other groups who said they could register 10,000 people for $20,000, when we could realistically project to register only 4,000 people for $20,000. The reality was that most of these $2 groups did not meet their goals. Eventually I spoke with an organizer from the national organization that had set the $2 standard and learned that the registration which had established the standard had been done in a large urban area, only once, and had never been possible to repeat. Experiences of this kind lead me to question why we are setting standards for ourselves that are impossible to meet, and why we aren't educating donors and foundations about what the real costs of social change work are.

In all these areas where I've argued that groups which work for social change need to get smart about organizing, I can also testify that PPP's strategies have not undermined our principles. We have learned how to work with the media, make long-range strategic plans, address the personal and financial needs of our staff, attend to fund-raising, budget development, and marketing, and work with foundations in ways that borrow from the world we are trying to change— but always in ways that send out our message of empowerment and economic justice.

10

·······················

What Happens
When We Begin to Win?

A
NY TIME AN ORGANIZATION achieves a victory and
begins challenging the status quo, there will be opposition and sometimes a serious backlash. Opposition
comes in many different forms, from ongoing criticism to
threats of violence and real harm. When PPP first experienced
serious opposition, it hit us unexpectedly. We didn't know
how to counter it. I think this kind of paralysis often happens
to social change organizations and that to avoid it we should
make preparation for opposition a part of our strategic planning. We need to plan to meet the opposition in positive ways,
so that we will not simply react in ways that may do us more
harm when it occurs.

At PPP, we have learned to plan for how we will deal with
opposition before the start of each new campaign. We look at
the ways that this campaign might be opposed and decide
what we should do in each of those cases. Every year, based on
our experiences, the list of possible ways we might be opposed
grows. For example, experience has taught us that during our

get-out-the-vote campaigns, we can be pretty sure that someone will try to tamper with the vehicles we rent to transport
voters to the polls. (This includes putting trash in the radia-
tors of our vans, including my own personal van.) So we plan
how we are going to protect our vehicles. Sometimes we scat-
ter them, parking them in different places, or sometimes we
hire a security guard to watch several vehicles at a time over-
night. Experience has also taught us to watch that our phone
lines don't get cut. During one election, we stopped getting
phone calls in the middle of the day at our "Get Out the Vote"
headquarters. We were so busy calling out we didn't notice at
first that we weren't receiving incoming calls; we just knew the
calls had slowed down and we wondered why. Finally, one of
our volunteers called on a different line. She said that she had
been trying to get through, but that all the other lines were
busy. Well, none of our phones had been ringing in our office,
so we called the phone company to report a problem. At first
they said they would take care of it. Later they said they
couldn't fix the problem until the next day. After we continued to complain, asked to speak to the manager, and threatened to call in the media, the phone company discovered how
to fix our lines. In the meantime, we had lost calls from folks
needing a ride to the polls.

The first step in dealing with opposition is to assume that
it will happen. It is so easy to deny that opposition will occur
because it is frightening to wait for it to hit. People close to
you and sometimes even members of your own group might
accuse you of being "paranoid." If you deny that opposition
will occur, your staff will be unprepared at a time when you
need to be most supportive of each other. At PPP, we now put
the issue of opposition on the agenda of our weekly meeting

so that it has become a "normal" topic for discussion. The second step in meeting opposition is to know how backlash will manifest itself. Those who oppose us might try to divide us by race, gender, or class, for instance. The third step is to understand that for every action or campaign, a response to the opposition must be prepared. The specific forms of opposition will change, but we can and must plan for all of them as part of developing a winning campaign.

PPP has had to deal with several levels of opposition. On one level, folks have been challenged as individuals. Many of our members have been challenged by others in the community who do not want them to continue their PPP work. Each time somebody steps forward to work for social justice of any kind, there will be personal consequences. Sometimes family members will not be supportive. Some of us at PPP have family members who are very conservative—some are even Klan members or supporters—who are very threatened by the work we do. Some of our members can no longer go to family reunions, or have been ostracized by their community and their church. One woman in our organization, who got involved through the Proctor-Silex campaign, suffered serious personal opposition after she began to take an active role in PPP. Her husband was very threatened by her choice and felt she should not be speaking out. He lost his temper frequently, argued with her, and even beat her a couple of times. Finally, when she continued to take a visible leadership role, he left her. One day, she came home to discover he had taken their trailer and left her homeless with three children. While this was devastating to her, she wrote us a letter to say she'd gained more than she had lost and did not regret her work with PPP on the plant closing. Another woman who has been active in

PPP was a leader in her church. After her work with PPP became known, people stopped talking to her and ignored her in public. It was a very subtle thing at first. When she continued to stay involved with PPP, she felt she had to leave the church community because of the painful rejection she had experienced. The church even removed the name of her mother, who was very ill and who had been a member of the church for many years, from the list of sick members for receiving get-well cards and visits.

People who have taken a visible role with PPP have also been threatened in their workplaces, have lost advancements they deserved, and have lost their jobs entirely. In a place like Kannapolis, North Carolina, the people who run the companies are often the people who are affiliated with traditional leadership. When PPP challenges one of the community's established leaders, it is not unusual for the people who run the companies in our community to retaliate against their employees. The woman I mentioned previously, whose husband opposed her involvement with PPP and who came home to find him gone and her trailer missing, was fired by Proctor-Silex for speaking out against the company. The wife of one of PPP's paid organizers (the couple had four children) was fired because the company she worked for was threatened by PPP's organizing activities. When you challenge the power structure, you will meet opposition from more than one corner because those in power always have friends in power.

Backlash from the companies in our community is not only directed at our members as individuals, but also at PPP as an organization. For example, a few years ago, when PPP was organizing a voter registration effort, we scheduled a Saturday fish fry. Fish fries are large community events where voter registration and education take place. Hundreds of people attend, and large numbers of volunteers work to organize and run the event. On the Thursday night before the Saturday event, every one of our volunteers who worked for a particular company got a call from their employer to say that they had to work on Saturday. Many people worked in different departments, and some of them had never worked on Saturday before. Other people in the same departments were not called in that day. It was a very direct attempt on the part of the company to stop this PPP event. In response, we asked each person who called us to say that they couldn't work for us on Saturday to find someone to volunteer in their place at our event. They did, and we were able to hold the fish fry.

Opposition to PPP has also used the media to discredit our organization and alienate our members. This has happened through direct attacks from the media but also in much more subtle ways. In June of 1988, I was shocked to read in a story in our local paper that a right-wing conservative candidate for Congress was the speaker at the 8th Congressional District Black Caucus Banquet sponsored by the Cabarrus County PPP volunteer coordinator. Not only was the candidate against all that we stood for, but PPP is a nonpartisan organization. When I called the Cabarrus County volunteer to discuss the story, she was equally shocked, because it was not true. That same week, a Richmond County paper listed a different PPP volunteer coordinator as the right-wing candidate's sponsor, and the Rowan County paper listed our volunteer coordinator from Rowan County as his sponsor. Similar stories linking our volunteers and this candidate continued to pop up in other county newspapers. None of these stories said anything about PPP directly, but all of them worked to discredit us with people who would know our volunteers and question their commitment. The media had not originated these stories. They had received press releases and printed them as usual.

The opposition may try to divide a group by pitting members against each other. I've related Midway's struggle for annexation by Aberdeen. After half of Midway had been improved with the help of a community development block grant, Aberdeen offered to annex the improved half only. When this happened the Midway residents felt angry and suspicious of each other, and a rift developed. PPP members immediately responded by urging everyone in the community to stick together and to continue to fight as a whole community for total annexation. If we had not been prepared to respond, this tactic might have destroyed the community group and the campaign.

Racism and homophobia have often been used to try to set our members at odds. People are divided on these issues anyway, and so they can easily be used to heighten tensions in a group. As I mentioned earlier, when PPP was trying to help Broadway residents get a community development block grant, a contractor told a Broadway resident, who was one of our steering committee members, that PPP should not be trusted because of our support for "homosexual rights." His strategy to alienate our steering committee member did not work because we had been open about our mission statement and had conducted workshops to prepare people for this kind of divisive tactic. We have also seen racial prejudice used to divide people, as when management in the plants tells employees that "foreign workers" are taking their jobs. If people are not adequately prepared to see how the opposition plays on common prejudices to divide and disempower them, they are often persuaded to abandon their common struggle. People who have joined with our organization as "allies" have also experienced opposition. In the early years of PPP, many middle-class people in our communities were involved in our organization. The same powerful forces in the community that threatened low-income people also threatened the middle-class people working with us. The backlash against middle-class people is usually more subtle. It often takes the form of criticism from members of their family or people in their churches or workplace. This type of opposition works by undermining the individual personally, discrediting PPP, or both. Recently, we took a group of middle-class folks who were participating in a PPP training program to a demonstration that was run by low-income folks. One of the participants reported that she had talked to the demonstrators and was very appalled at their living conditions. She said she had been moved and energized by the stories she heard and wanted to figure out how to work with the people she had met. But the next morning, someone in her church told her that she didn't have the whole story and raised questions about the people doing the organizing. Rather than question this person, she quickly allowed herself to doubt and discredit everything she had heard at the demonstration. She did continue in PPP training, and later she recognized how she had been side-tracked from her own perceptions by the beliefs of someone with the "credibility" of her own privileged class background.

Helping people recognize and understand the different forms opposition takes is critical to surviving it. At PPP, we have developed specific strategies to counter the different kinds of opposition that we encounter, both as an organization and as individuals. In organizing campaigns, we always lay out the things that might happen to divide us or stop our work. We talk to a new group of volunteers about how people can be pulled away from the organization by bribes or favors. We let people in the community know that others may try to separate us and how they may go about it. We explain that those in power often prefer us to fight among ourselves rather than against the power structure.

At the beginning of every PPP campaign, we identify one organizer who is specifically available to deal with emergency problems. This person's job is to focus on the opposition and develop contingency plans that will help us respond immediately to emergency situations. This person is the one we turn to if the phones stop working or a van is sabotaged. We always have lawyers on standby to help us with legal emergencies. In the 1990 election we actually had a mechanic on standby, and before the polls opened we made certain we knew where we could get tires because during a past election someone had slashed our tires. These are some of the forms opposition can take in rural North Carolina.

Also at the beginning of each campaign, we try to anticipate the backlash that will follow if we succeed in our goals. We sit down together and brainstorm about security for the organization and for individual members. We develop plans so that we feel prepared to deal with any contingencies. This has been a very important part of our planning because, even if things happen that we are not prepared for, we have gotten our fears out in the open and agreed that we will work together to stop the backlash, rather than let it overwhelm us.

Building an understanding of backlash is something we begin long before any specific campaign. It is explored in all of our trainings and workshops. In a Building Bridges training exercise, for instance, we asked a group of middle-income and wealthy people to talk about how they have experienced backlash. They told many stories. Some were about subtle forms of backlash; for example, of people discrediting them by telling them they were just being naive or that poor people don't want them involved. Some stories were about more painful experiences. They talked about being "iced out" of family situations when they raised political topics or of just living in complete silence among their families about their involvement. They talked about their children saying that they were embarrassed and that they didn't want their parents to continue their commitment. And some stories indicated backlash that threatened their social and possibly their economic status. They talked, for instance, about social pressure from people in their congregations and disapproval from their ministers. Sharing these stories helped legitimize their experience of backlash. We asked the workshop participants to act out a conversation with the person who most tries to undermine them. Through this experience many of these middle-class participants were able to recognize how they are pulled away or are made to feel guilty about the work they are doing. Facing up to the backlash reenacted through these conversations helped them learn how to respond in ways that preserve their feelings of self-worth.

In Finding Our Voices training, we often find that the low-income people in the training group are very embarrassed or ashamed to talk about what happens to them in their church or with their families or, particularly, on the job as a result of their PPP work. But once a conversation gets started, often by a staff person who shares a story about an embarrassing or painful experience of backlash, the low-income people are encouraged to speak up. In training people we let them know that if we are successful at making changes, we are going to get opposition. *If we are not getting opposition, then we must not be doing enough!*

The most important way in which an organization prepares for opposition is by creating a community of support. We at PPP talk a lot about building a healthy "family" within our organization. And, as anyone knows, a healthy family is one where members grow, change, learn, and respect each other's differences. Every year at PPP we meet as a staff and talk about the ways in which we want to have better personal lives. Then we try as a group to shape our work in ways that fit our own personal goals as well as our goals for the organization. We try to make sure that the work of PPP will not tear us away from ourselves, but instead is work that will help to build who we are. That is the only kind of work that will strengthen us enough, year after year, to overcome the opposition.

We have shaped PPP to be an organization that celebrates the connections between people's lives. We recognize and honor each other in as many ways as we possibly can. Our celebrations are not just for our organizing victories, but also to affirm our personal strength.

When I first started to write this chapter, I thought about calling it "Backlash" or "Opposition," but I realized that would be the wrong thing to emphasize. At PPP, we have found a way to turn the negative and all too real experience of opposition into a way of building community with each other and more support for our work together. Preparing for opposition is just one more step in building a family and a community that will stand together to face what comes after we begin to win.

....

Building Unity
for Real Democracy

IN ORDER TO write this book, I left North Carolina and
moved to Concord, Massachusetts, for a year. I was appointed as a Public Policy Fellow at Radcliffe College. It
was the first time I had lived out of the South and the first time
I had lived in a middle-class community. In the beginning I
was terrified. I knew I would have to deal with class prejudice,
especially working in an advanced academic setting when I
had no college degree. I was afraid that my own feelings of inferiority would not allow me to function in this setting, that I
would be in a constant state of "shutdown." I was afraid that
living in that setting would make me feel bad about myself all
the time.

And, in fact, that did happen to me in the beginning. Not
because people intended to make me feel bad. In fact, the response and support I got from most people was wonderful,
but if only one person, even unknowingly, said something that
ruined my self-esteem, I would forget the support of all the
others. This happened often, and I found myself constantly

struggling to remember that I did have something to offer. I was unable to write until these feelings began to change.

In April of 1993, I made a formal public presentation at the Bunting Institute of Radcliffe College. This was the first time I had put my own ideas out in a formal structured way. I had done lots of presentations about the work of the Piedmont Peace Project, but I had never publicly laid out my own theories and ideas about social change and how to make it happen. I wasn't sure how people would react. I didn't know if people would be able to understand my thinking or believe my experiences. In fact, they did. The response was very positive. There were some people who didn't like what I had to say, and I struggled with that, but I focused on the fact that what I was saying was important and that many people really understood. That experience helped me begin writing.

The process of writing this book has forced me to learn to communicate my ideas and my visions. A lot of times, I came up against ideas that I wanted to communicate, but didn't have the language for. That's part of my struggle even now. It has been a struggle to figure out how to get enough of my thoughts down, to get my ideas into words, into language that others can understand. It has been a real challenge. It's meant I've had to learn new ways to talk about the issues I care about most.

Along the way, I've also learned a lot about my ability to deal with those bad feelings about myself that I thought I would always have to struggle to overcome. During my year in Concord I've realized that I don't always feel bad about myself. I don't always question my own intelligence, and I am no longer reluctant to identify myself as lesbian. I do sometimes panic—someone can say something that sends me running back to that doubtful place immediately. But it's not a constant battle anymore. Living in a middle-class and academic community for a year, I have come to see more clearly than ever before that *each* of us—low-income, middle-class, and wealthy, women and men, people of color and white, heterosexual, gay, and lesbian, academics and non–formally educated folks—has resources that are important for breaking down barriers and building a movement for social change.

When I first began knowing that I wanted to be an organizer, I would keep going back to a passage in a Quaker guidebook. The passage said that social change has always happened because one person or a few people had a vision and set about to make it happen. While I did not fully believe in the beginning that one person, or a few people, can make a difference, I did have a strong feeling that I wanted to do something, and I also had a vision. My vision was to live in a world where everyone's basic needs would be met—housing, health care, food, clothing, and all levels of education. People would be respected and honored for their differences. Disagreements and violations would be dealt with in fair and nonviolent ways. It would be a world without the threat of self-destruction from nuclear weapons. It would be a world where the environment was preserved. A world where all voices would be heard.

I now look back over the past ten years and believe that one person *can* make a difference. Not alone, but by building a movement where the vision continues to grow, and includes people from all different walks of life. If we can help people believe in themselves, believe that they personally can make a difference, then we will be able to build a movement that will change the world.

Just as one person can't make changes without organizing

and mobilizing other people, organizations can't make the changes they want by themselves either.

Even though I always knew that building a successful social change movement requires bridging class and race lines, I didn't always believe it could happen. My own experience with class prejudices and the feelings of inferiority they generated in me made me doubt the possibility. But, just as I knew I had to learn to believe in myself and to speak for myself, even though at first I didn't think I could, I also knew I had to believe in the possibility of building across class lines. There was some deep knowing in me that this belief was right. I now know, based on my personal experience, that these alliances *are* possible to build. I don't have to doubt or distrust that it can happen. The work isn't easy and nothing happens without both sides constantly working hard to build a strong bridge that will endure. And the rewards are great.

I hope that low-income people and organizers for social change will learn from this book that these alliances can be built without sacrificing the principles of our organizations. It *is* possible for low-income people to work with middle-class and wealthy people without having to "adapt" or change who they are. An alliance *can* be built that brings middle-class people into a movement in ways that support low-income people and their ideas.

I hope all readers of this book will begin to think about building community in very broad ways. We must remember what it means to have a true community and how rewarding that can be. Building organizations that respect individual struggles while also organizing politically ("the personal is political") is building community. Community is what has made PPP successful. Personal connections have made us strong—strong enough to be able to stay together and move forward even during times of internal conflicts and tremendous opposition.

My biggest hope for all readers of this book is that they realize that we must look at the systems that cause our social problems in the first place. The challenge is much greater than just finding temporary solutions to deal with single problems. We must all begin to see the place of our work in the context of the social justice movement and to work in our different ways toward its goals if we are going to build a real democracy in a just and peaceful world.

So where do we go from here?

In the fall of 1995, I left the Piedmont Peace Project to become the director of the Peace Development Fund, a national organization that strengthens grassroots social change organizations through grants and training. In addition to building the capacity of community organizing groups, the Peace Development Fund works to support and strengthen the progressive social change movement. I am bringing to my new work my vision and experience rooted in the Piedmont Peace Project to connect with and support similar work across the United States. All of us who work for social change and to bring about real democracy are needed in the effort to determine where, as a nation, we go from here. We are in a serious crisis at this point in our history, and I believe that unless we begin to act immediately, our visions and hopes for the future will never happen.

In this book I have discussed many ways I believe that we must begin to work differently as a society in order to build a true community. In addition, I believe that we must begin to work toward a long-term collective vision of changing the world.

First, I would ask you to stop and think about your own vision of the kind of world you would like to live in. Imagine what a day in that world would be like for you, for your children, and for their children. This is where social change begins.*

As individuals, we must discover which organizations and groups meet the long-term vision that we hold, and then commit ourselves to working with those groups toward that vision. I've stressed in this book that it is important to remember that social change work is difficult, time-consuming, and usually an uphill struggle. As a result, in their commitment to social change, individuals must create plans that respect their personal needs and abilities. Otherwise, they will not be with us for the long haul.

Real democracy cannot be achieved through the efforts of any single national organization or because of a political third party, although these forces are essential to the struggle. I believe that a successful revolution has to begin at the grassroots, door to door, with everyone sharing in the vision and leadership.

Beginning at the grassroots means that every organization must develop a long-term strategic plan for realizing its vision—I suggest twenty-five years. This plan is one that explains what we want for our lives individually and in community and says where we want to be as an organization. It should be about building economically, socially, environmen-

---

* See the Appendix for a "25-Year Vision Exercise" that has been used successfully in training workshops to help participants begin to see their own visions of a better world.

tally, and politically sustainable communities. It should consider how we work to achieve the plan nationally as well as locally. It should include our ideas on how to prepare new leadership who will be accountable to the people who elect them. And it should make clear how we have redefined the positions of power these representatives will assume. Finally, all groups should compare and revise their plans until a relationship between them emerges that will work for world change.

I am not suggesting that any one group quit working on their own issues or with their own community. But I do think that all of our work needs to be seen in the context of a larger mission, and that we must always keep that larger goal in focus. For example, the Peace Development Fund staff and board are working on creating a long-term, twenty-five-year vision for our work. As we develop our program and fundraising plans for the coming year, we keep that vision in focus and observe carefully to see how our current plans work toward it.

Imagine sitting down to do your yearly budget and fundraising plan knowing where you want to be in five years, ten years, twenty-five years. Rethinking expenditures of time and energy and money in this way may lead you in new directions. For example, developing youth leadership becomes critical when thinking about where you want to be twenty-five years down the road. We all need to count on having strong committed leaders that far into the future. You may also rethink your criteria for choosing your group and coalition affiliations. You'll ask yourself, "Does our work with this group move us toward our long-term vision?" And if the answer is yes, you'll want to map out clearly your shared strategy for the future.

Sometimes managing the coalition of just a few groups is

difficult work, so that the idea of bringing together all social change groups, first regionally, then nationally, and finally internationally, to create a common vision for world change may seem a phenomenal task. But I believe it can be accomplished. And I would like to say that our present way of working for social change, in separate and competing groups and without a shared long-term plan, is highly ineffective.

As I envision it, this national coalition, or unity group, would be made up of representatives of truly diverse groups. The unity group must include a majority of strong voices of low-income people, people of color, and women. This is necessary to ensure that everyone has an equal voice, that folks who live with oppression play a critical role in creating a new future. I don't believe it is possible for any one organization to lead the unity group. Too much competition for funds and leadership exists for a single organization to lead effectively. Instead, the unity group should hire and supervise staff who will work for the best interest of all groups involved. Agreements would have to be worked out around how finances would be raised, how day-to-day management is carried out, and how all groups involved get an equal voice in decision making and shaping the common vision.

I believe the proper and achievable goal of such a unity group would be to build a new world—a world that honors people over money, a world with true equality and justice, where everyone is guaranteed a living wage, housing, education, and health care.

I would like to close this book by offering some ideas on what a successful unity plan should include:

1. A look at the history of revolutionary movements within this country and others, to figure out what worked well in the

past and what we need to do differently in context of current times.

2. A strategic marketing plan. This would include a media plan that not only supported the work and vision of individual groups, and promoted the vision to the larger public, but would also work toward our goals of developing a strong voice within current media structures and creating alternative structures when needed.

3. A political vision. We will need to figure out what a political structure should look like and how we begin to train future political leaders. There are people both within and outside of the current political structure who would be invaluable resources in helping create this piece of the vision.

4. Training of new organizers with a special emphasis on developing organizers from low-income communities and folks who would work within their own communities.

5. A political leadership institute that would train people to run the country under this new vision. They would need to learn alternative methods of leadership, economic development, and peaceful negotiations and security, as well as have an understanding of economics, international affairs, and consumer affairs.

6. Resource development. We need to begin now to develop resources that are not dependent on foundations or people who might not agree with our vision.

7. Many people in the social change movement do not believe we can make any change without major campaign reform and more participation and access to voting. I agree. On the other hand, I do not believe we can achieve these reforms without a much larger movement behind us. So, while I believe that fighting for these reforms must be among our early

goals, I do not believe we should wait for them to happen before moving forward with a plan.

8. Peaceful ways to deal with opposition. As I've said before, when we begin to win, we will be met with opposition. We need to be prepared as a movement to take a peaceful but proactive stand against such opposition. We must teach groups and individuals how to deal with the opposition they will face through peaceful means of protecting themselves.

We will have many visions of what a just and equitable democracy will look like, and we will have even more ideas on how to get there. But we must begin to work together, to compromise, and to listen to each other in order to realize our visions. Working together will be the hardest challenge we will face. Much harder than facing the opposition or working alone. But it is the only way we will win. It is the only way to create revolutionary change.

25-Year Vision Exercise

THE FOLLOWING is an exercise I have used to help participants begin to see their own personal long-term visions of a better world. The exercise helps individuals express their own visions and also work in a group to develop alternative plans (brainstorm) for realizing their visions. When working as a group, the rule of brainstorming is that everyone's view is listed, even if one person's view is contradictory to another person's view. People in the group should not argue with each other about an idea or vision during the brainstorming process. These arguments can occur later when participants actually begin to develop plans. The time periods given in parentheses are guidelines for a group of six to ten people. These times can be adjusted to meet a group's needs.

Step 1. Add twenty-five years to your age and write it down. Think of the child or children closest to you and add twenty-five years to their ages. Write their names and ages down. (These children might be daughters, sons, nieces, nephews, grandchildren, friends, pupils.) (15 minutes)

Step 2. Think about a day twenty-five years from now. The year is 2021 (do your own math!). You get up on that morning and check on the news. You get a call from the child (or children) you listed in step 1, who is now an adult and wants to talk to you about what he or she is doing. You walk out into your community, and you can appreciate all of the hard work you've done most of your life to create this community—this world that you are now living in. Your vision of living in a just and peaceful world, a clean and fruitful environment, has come to pass because of all your hard work. Just sit for a few minutes and imagine what that world looks like and how it feels. Draw a picture or write a description of what you see. (10–15 minutes)

Step 3. Turn to the person next to you. You are still in the year 2021, and you haven't seen this person in a long time. Talk about what you are doing now. Describe your work and what you are interested in. Tell what the children in your life are doing as adults. Talk about what you are most pleased about having accomplished over the past twenty-five years. (10 minutes)

Step 4. List the things that were different in the future world that you imagined from the way they are now. Remember, we have accomplished your dream! (10 minutes)

Step 5. Brainstorm: What has happened in our society to make our visions of the future become a reality? Write down everyone's ideas. Make a timeline of the changes you imagine have occurred. (15 minutes)

Step 6. Brainstorm: What do we need as an organization to be able to make this vision a reality? Write down everyone's ideas. (15 minutes)

Step 7. Brainstorm: What do you need as an individual in order to participate actively in this work for the next twenty-five years? Write down everyone's ideas. (15 minutes)

Library of Congress Cataloging-in-Publication Data

Stout, Linda.

    Bridging the class divide and other lessons for grassroots organizing / Linda Stout ; with a foreword by Howard Zinn.

      p.   cm.

    Includes bibliographical references and index.

    ISBN 0-8070-4309-5 (cloth)

    1. Social problems—United States.   I. Title.

HN65.S75   1996

361.1'0973—dc20   96-18150